P9-BJQ-541

Lose the Halo, Keep the Wings

Great Advice for Ministers' Wives

Virginia L. Wilson

New Hope
Birmingham, Alabama

New Hope
P. O. Box 12065
Birmingham, AL 35202-2065 ·

©1996 by New Hope
All rights reserved. First printing 1996
Printed in the United States of America

Dewey Decimal Classification: 253.2
Subject Headings: CLERGY—SPOUSES
      CHRISTIAN LIFE—WOMEN
      CLERGY—FAMILY LIFE
      WOMEN IN THE CHURCH
      WOMEN IN CHURCH WORK

Scripture quotations indicated by NASB are taken from the NEW AMERICAN STANDARD BIBLE®, © Copyright The Lockman Foundation 1960, 1962, 1963, 1968, 1971, 1972, 1973, 1975, 1977. Used by permission.

Scripture quotations indicated by NIV are from the Holy Bible, New International Version. Copyright ©1973, 1978, 1984 International Bible Society. Used by permission of Zondervan Bible Publishers.

Scripture quotations indicated by NKJV are from the Holy Bible, New King James Version. Copyright ©1979, 1980, 1982 by Thomas Nelson, Inc. Used by permission.

Scripture quotations indicated by KJV are from the King James Version of the Bible.

Scripture quotation indicated by NRSV is from the *New Revised Standard Version of the Bible,* Copyright ©1989 by the Division of Christian Education of the National Council of the Churches of Christ in the USA. Used by permission. All rights reserved.

Cover design by Janell E. Young
Cover illustration and inside illustrations by Kelly Smith

ISBN: 1-56309-116-X
N964126•0696•5M1

Contents

Introduction

"You want to go back to school and prepare for what? The 'ministry!' What in the world is a ministry? I didn't hear about that before, during, or even after the wedding ceremony! Do I have to be included in this ministry?"

These were only a few of the questions I had for Gene when he announced that he felt God had called him into the ministry when he was 17 years old. We had been married for 3 years. This was a minor detail he had forgotten to tell me *before* we were married! How could he do this to me? He was such a successful businessman, rising rapidly in his company. What a change this was going to make in our lives! I wasn't ready for a change like this. I had never imagined in my wildest dreams that I would ever become a minister's wife. But, I am getting ahead of myself. I really should begin at the beginning.

My entrance into the unique life of a minister's wife was backwards. My life has never been normal, whatever normal is. All the big events in my life have been unusual. But even though I have done most things backwards, the Lord has straightened them out for His glory.

I was different. I certainly didn't fit any mold or stereotype of the "perfect minister's wife." For that matter, I still don't. But I did finally find a wonderful peace in becoming the person God designed me to be and I found joy in ministering with the husband God gave me.

I have had the privilege of serving as a minister's wife for 20 years in Texas, the wife of a director of missions for 5 years in the Los Angeles area, and the wife of the Illinois Baptist State Association executive director whose responsibility it was to minister to more than 1,000 churches in the state. By the way, I have been married to the same man

while he fulfilled all of these positions! All have been chal-
lenging and all have been different.

Being a minister's wife has been full of joy, anguish,
happiness, heartache, love, forgiveness, beauty, and awe,
just to name a few emotions. I didn't choose this life for
myself, but looking back, I wouldn't trade it for any other. I
have learned that our Lord does not prepare the easiest way
for us, but the best. God does not use the strong for his
work here on earth, but the weak. He mounts us "on wings
like eagles" so we can "run and not grow weary, . . . walk
and not be faint" (Isa. 40:31 NIV). The Lord became my
strength, my resting place, my wisdom, my future.

As my husband, Gene, and I have traveled across the
United States, Canada, and Puerto Rico, I have heard ministers' wives express the same concerns. We are all looking
for peace and joy in discovering who we are as the women
of God. We don't want to be stereotyped; we want people to
love us for who we are. We want to be real people in a real
world. We want to find satisfaction in using our gifts where
God has planted us.

My prayer is that the Lord will bless and warm your
heart as you read the following pages. I hope through the
unfolding of my life's experiences serving Christ, you will
understand more fully how you can best serve God alongside your husband. Then, with a new confidence you will
go forth rejoicing and touching lives for Christ.

Part 1

Knowing Yourself and God's Plan for You

1

Listen and Learn

My first experiences as a minister's wife were full of blunders! I can look back now and laugh; but at the time it was often painful. I was young and naive. The following incident will give you a little clue about the extent of my inexperience as a minister's wife.

Gene had accepted his first pastorate in Ida, Louisiana. We were also full-time students at a college in Marshall, Texas, and we both worked part-time jobs. One Sunday after church, we were having lunch with Mr. and Mrs. Snow. They had an unusual home that was actually on the borderline of two states. Their kitchen was in Louisiana and their bedroom was in Arkansas. After the meal, we moved to the living room to continue our visit. The conversation naturally turned to farming, which was the main occupation of the men in that area. This brand-new minister's wife, all of 23 years old, listened eagerly as the seasoned farmer discussed *planting by the moon.* Being a city girl, I found this concept fascinating and I contemplated this unfamiliar term of *planting by the moon* for a whole ten seconds. Then I blurted out, "That's strange. I've never seen anyone planting their crops at night." All eyes turned on me. What had I said? The old farmer looked at me with an astonished expression on his furrowed brow. Rising slowly, he walked to his bookcase and carefully lifted a book from the shelf. It was a farmer's almanac. I had never seen one before.

This sensitive man proceeded to explain what planting by the moon meant. In a steady voice, Mr. Snow gave me my first lesson in planting crops according to the moon, the tides, and the seasons, just as though I were one of his beloved grandchildren. This city girl and new minister's wife learned a lot that day. My biggest lesson—listen and learn!

So You're Not Sure You Want to Be a Minister's Wife!

Perhaps you really don't like serving beside your minister husband. You are not exactly sure that being a part of ministry with your husband is your cup of tea. You haven't received any preparation or training. Maybe you are just starting your journey as a minister's wife with fear and trembling, not knowing what to expect. How do you live up to everyone's expectations? Maybe you have gone to seminary; and after a few years of service with your husband, you have become disillusioned by it all. Maybe you are a veteran minister's wife who is tired of people always expecting so much from you.

You could be the wife of a minister who serves a denomination in an associational or state ministry. These ministers, as well as men who are evangelists, spend much time on the road. You can grow tired of your husband having little time with you or the children, and you have had it!

I really haven't been reading your mail. I've been there. I understand how you feel about these areas of your life. The following chapters will show you how God has answered many of these questions and used me in ministering to others in spite of myself.

Discussion Starters

1. What position does your husband have in ministry?

2. Did you know before you married that your knight in shining armor was going to be a minister? If not, when and how did he make the announcement?

3. Did you plan to marry a minister? Did it work out the way you planned?

4. Are you just getting started as a minister's wife? How long has your husband been serving and in what positions?

5. Have you had an embarrassing experience as a young minister's wife? Share some of your early experiences.

2

Backward Beginnings

High School Sweethearts

Everyone in school knew how tough my father was because he taught many of the students in the fourth grade. Daddy became a principal by the time I was in high school. For some reason, all the boys in school were afraid of my father. Not only was he their principal, but they had heard he would put them through an inquisition before they could date me.

Gene was the first brave young man to take the challenge. He asked me out because of a dare. I didn't find out until 2 years later. It seemed that a fellow football player extended the dare to Gene one afternoon and Gene took him up on it. After memorizing his speech, Gene telephoned me and asked, "Could I please have the honor of escorting you to the senior graduation banquet at my church?" Who could resist such a gracious invitation? I was so impressed with Gene's polite manner that I told him I would call him back as soon as possible with my reply. I rushed to my father to ask for permission. My father was not only a principal but he was a general in the army reserves. Needless to say, he often carried his authoritative methods into our home. Daddy said he would have to meet this young man before I could go out with him.

When Gene and my father finally got together for the

question-and-answer ordeal, Gene appeared undaunted. Daddy liked that in a young man. Having all of his questions answered satisfactorily, Daddy agreed for Gene to escort me to his church graduation banquet.

After 2 years of dating, Gene proposed to me. His personality and charm gradually won me over. I fell deeply in love with this strong man with a tender heart.

Overcoming an Obstacle

Before we could marry, we had one obstacle to overcome. Gene belonged to one denomination and I belonged to another. We felt that it was important to worship together in the same church after we were married. But which church? We decided to visit each other's church and then make our decision. I was in for a big surprise!

Walking into Gene's church was like walking into a beehive. Men and women were chattering, hugging, and laughing out loud. It was certainly overwhelming for this quiet-natured girl. What a contrast to my church services. When the service ended, I sprinted out the church door to get to the car. Gene could barely keep up with me as he rushed to open the door.

Thoughtfully looking into my eyes, he waited for my evaluation of the service. Not wanting to hurt his feelings, I gathered as much courage as I could and blurted out what I was thinking.

"I really don't think I can ever go back into that church again. The preacher preached too loudly, the people talked too much, the musicians played too loudly, and I didn't know any of the songs. While we're on the subject, why did that preacher have to walk around so much on the platform while he was preaching? Why didn't he stay behind the pulpit?"

Gene walked around to the driver's side of the car and slid in. I repeated my initial statement for emphasis, in case Gene hadn't caught it the first time. "Gene, I'm sorry; but I really don't think I can ever go back into that church again!"

Without saying a word, Gene smiled and backed the car

out of the parking lot. Nothing more was said. I raised my eyebrow in the silence and looked at Gene out of the corner of one eye. He seemed undisturbed by my last statement; I sighed with relief thinking, *That wasn't so hard. It's all settled. I'm glad we don't have to deal with this church issue anymore. I'll never go back to that church again.*

I'm sure, however, at that moment the Lord was chuckling with amusement as He listened to my adamant statement. The Lord knew that Gene had been mentored by the preacher I had so vehemently rejected that day. In fact, the Lord knew Gene would turn out to preach just like that man. Many surprises lay in store for us in the years ahead! But the Lord was compassionate; He did not let me see my future. He patiently gave me time to get ready for my life as a minister's wife.

Love Conquers All—The Nuptials Are Pronounced

Gene and I were engaged as I began my second semester of college. The trauma of visiting Gene's church and the skepticism of his denomination had eased. We found a wonderful little church in our college town that just happened to be Gene's denomination. Each Sunday we sat listening to the preacher. He was soft-spoken and I liked that! The love in the church and the spirit in the message gradually warmed my heart. I decided to become a member of this friendly denomination.

On July 23, 1965, Gene and I were married in Thomas Avenue Church in Pasadena, Texas. The wedding was beautiful and the church was packed with loving friends and relatives. We had a wonderful reception, and then were escorted off on our honeymoon amid a shower of rice.

The first year of our marriage I found that although Gene was spending an enormous amount of time working in the retail business, he didn't seem to enjoy it. So I began praying for him. Little did I know that God was going to answer those innocent prayers in a phenomenal way. After 3 years of marriage, Gene came home from work one day and said, "Virginia, I believe that the Lord wants me to go back to school and prepare for the ministry."

"What ministry?" I said. "I never knew about a ministry." Astonished by his announcement, I asked why he didn't mention this to me while we were dating. With my mind still swirling in confusion, I defiantly asked Gene, "Does the wife have to be a part of this ministry? If she does, I never signed on for this. I never saw it in the fine print of our marriage certificate. What a mean trick!"

All along I was thinking, *So this is what I get for praying for Gene. God, why didn't You warn me about this when I was praying for him anyway?* The Lord's loving response was, "Virginia, you asked Me to make Gene happy and give him what he needed to make his life complete, didn't you?"

"Well, yes, Lord, but I never dreamed it would be something like *ministry!*" As Gene was speaking about ministry, the Lord put His arms around me and gave me His peace.

Calming myself, I responded to the Lord, "I know You love me and You love Gene. I guess it is silly of me to get so worked up over a little word like *ministry.*"

Slowly I placed my life in the Master's hands. I decided to relax and let the Lord have control. I began to understand that ministry was not as frightening as I had thought. As I began to trust God with this new decision, I felt secure in His care.

Gene, with his convincing manner, tried to explain what preparation for the ministry was all about. I agreed to go back to school and finish my education as Gene prepared for his ministry. Gene knew what he was supposed to do, but I didn't have a clue.

After completing our arrangements to enter college, Gene and I said good-bye to our families, friends, and full-time jobs. We journeyed to Marshall, Texas, one sweltering August day with all of our worldly possessions packed in a rental truck. We had trekked across what we considered foreign country to our unknown future. Our first day in Marshall, we registered for classes, found part-time jobs, and located a place to live.

As an "older" married couple (I was 24 and Gene was 26), the students on the campus treated us with great respect. They held doors open for us and called us ma'am and sir. It was really quite comical. We met many other married couples going to college and are still good friends with many of them.

Once again I was doing everything backwards, but somehow God was straightening it out. I married a man who asked me out on a dare. I thought I was marrying a man who would work in retail all his life. After 3 years of marriage, my husband tells me he wants to become a minister. I worked at a secular job and then went back to school with my husband. What a strange turn of events. Nothing was happening the way I had planned it. But it's good to know that God can straighten things out as long as we are working with Him.

Our years of going to college as married students formed some of the happiest memories of our marriage. It was fun going to classes together, studying, and meeting other couples who were preparing to serve the Lord too. Each Sunday Gene and I traveled to the little east Texas churches as he filled in for the pastors when they were away. We were tithing for the first time in our marriage. I loved sitting in the pew listening to Gene preach. I could see a marked improvement in his messages every Sunday. During those days, we had the opportunity to meet some of God's choicest people, people who had been serving God faithfully for years. Life wasn't so difficult after all; that is, until certain impossible demands started being placed on me.

Expectations—Theirs, Mine, or God's?

In college, I was majoring in sociology and minoring in English. However, I wasn't taking any courses that prepared me for my responsibilities as a minister's wife. But the Lord had me in "on-the-job training" as we traveled to different churches. I am a fast learner and it didn't take me long to find out the east Texas stereotype of a good minister's wife. She was a woman who could play the piano with finesse, who knew every hymn and its page number by heart, and who could sing a stirring solo with no prior notice. These expectations became a humorous, repetitive scene as we stepped into a different church building early each Sunday morning and exchanged greetings with the leadership.

Predictably, either the head deacon or the head of the women's missions organization would vigorously shake my hand and at the same time anxiously ask if I played the piano. Before giving me an opportunity to respond, he or she would explain how desperately they needed a pianist or how beautifully the former minister's wife had played. When the greeter finally took a breath, I would rather sheepishly reply, "I can't play the piano at all. As a matter of fact, I can't even play the radio without getting static."

This was supposed to be a joke; but it often fell on unsympathetic ears. Oh, they were nice enough to me; but it was evident that I would never receive their vote for minister's wife of the year. They seemed to think I was absolutely useless since I couldn't play the piano or sing a solo. Because of this rejection, I began a search to find who I was and what I thought my responsibilities were as a minister's wife.

Looking frantically through the Bible for a set of rules on how to be a good minister's wife, I found none. There were no rules chiseled in stone like the Ten Commandments. What I found was that God didn't make a distinction between Christian women and minister's wives, but He did have some definite things to say to all wives in 1 Timothy 3:11 (NASB). We are to "be dignified, not malicious gossips, but temperate, faithful in all things." Women are to follow the teachings in 1 Timothy 2, 1 Peter 3, and Proverbs 31. These and many other Scripture passages gave me ample guidelines to follow. I tried following and obeying these Scriptures, but somehow the leadership in those churches felt I should also exhibit musical abilities. Musical ability was certainly missing in my life, so what could I do?

Discussion Starters

1. Where and how did you and your husband meet and fall in love?

2. Did your husband go to a special school for training?

3. Did you receive any special training to prepare for the ministry? If so, what kind?

4. Did any of the early churches you and your husband served have a stereotyped image of a minister's wife? If so, what did they expect? How did you cope?

3

The Cart Before the Horse

Because I sensed something was missing in my life as a minister's wife, I started searching for the answers. Could it be that I was doing things backwards again? Had I put the cart before the horse?

I went to catechism faithfully for 2 years as a teenager and learned a great deal about the Bible and God. I had always loved the Lord. I had been taught that if I was kind to my neighbor, went to church, and read my Bible, *maybe* I could go to heaven.

While in college I did my first individual study of the Scriptures. As a result of that study, I began to question the teachings of my denomination and decided to join Gene's denomination.

One Sunday I walked down the aisle at the end of the service to join his church. The preacher asked me if I knew the Lord. I looked at him with a blank stare and said, "Yes, I have always known the Lord." My response should have indicated that I had not experienced repentance and a new life in Christ. Instead of asking me to share my salvation experience with him, however, he gave me a card to complete. The congregation voted to receive me as a member of the church and I was baptized.

Gene pastored a small church during our last year of college. Then, we moved to Fort Worth, Texas, where Gene enrolled in seminary. Of course, we found a church there to attend.

The church in Fort Worth was different from other churches I had known. People in this church were always praising the Lord and sharing their testimonies with one another. They expressed such excitement about the Lord. We were impressed with what we saw and heard. Until then, I had never heard a testimony from a Christian. Members told of how they had come to know the Lord and accept Him as personal Savior.

We joined the church and became active members. I was fascinated by the testimonies I heard and began searching for a testimony of my own. I didn't want to appear different. I thought back to the time I joined another church and heard Jesus calling my name. With a few embellishments, that became my testimony.

Of course, my problem wasn't whether I had a testimony, but rather whether I had a relationship with Christ. I knew there was no in-between. If Jesus was to return, I wanted to be certain I would be counted in the number that would return to heaven with Him.

I began praying and making bargains with God. When we had outreach activities, I would ask the Lord to allow me to lead someone to Christ. If I could lead someone to Christ, surely I must be saved! Following such an encounter I would feel relief and continue serving the Lord with a partial sense of peace. Before long, however, the question of repentance would tug at my heart again and the doubts would surface. This struggle continued for about 2 years.

The Lord finally ended my dilemma in a most unusual way. Gene and I were at a Bible camp in Myrtle, Mississippi, with another couple, Mary Lynn and Jim. The first night we were there I had the opportunity to lead Mary Lynn to the Lord. I had been praying for her for some time.

The next afternoon we gathered in the sanctuary for a time of offering. I walked forward to place my offering on the altar. As I started back to my seat, I saw an old friend in the congregation. Wilma, a former Sunday School teacher of mine, motioned for me to sit with her for a moment; she wanted to introduce me to a friend. The young woman Wilma introduced me to was a minister's wife too. In addition, she had grown up with a minister for a father.

Briefly, the woman shared her testimony with me. For years she had been troubled about whether she was lost or saved. Finally, the previous year at this Bible camp she had prayed a prayer, "Lord, I can't continue this quizzing game. I want You to show me before this next service is over whether I am lost or saved." The young woman smiled at me and said, "And do you know what, Virginia? The Lord showed me before that service was over that I was lost. I did not have a relationship with Christ. I went forward last year at this Bible camp, repented of my sins, and asked Christ to be my Savior. It has been so wonderful because I have had such peace since then."

The young woman asked me to share my testimony with her. Briefly I told her of my previous experience. Then she asked me a curious question, "Virginia, have you always had peace about your salvation?"

I looked at her with a shocked expression. How did she know I had been struggling with doubts for the past 2 years? *It's none of her business,* I thought. *I'm not going to share my innermost secrets with a perfect stranger. It's really none of her business!*

Smiling, I carefully replied to her question with an emphatic, "Yes! Yes, I have peace about my salvation."

Inside, my heart was pounding. *I've got to get away from this woman,* I thought. *I don't want to talk to her anymore.* As quickly as possible, I told her how glad I was to have met her and left.

When the afternoon service ended, we walked to the dining hall for dinner. Gene and I took our places at a table. With dismay, I realized we sat down beside that same minister's wife! Her husband was with her now. He was praising the Lord in exuberant shouts.

Normally I love being around people who boldly express their faith, but at that moment I was turned off. Then I felt something strange come over me. The more the minister and his wife talked about the Lord, the more I felt like I was made of glass. I imagined that everyone in that dining hall could see right through me. For the first time in my life I felt like a hypocrite.

I didn't understand what was happening to me. I just knew I had to get out of that dining hall and away from that woman. When the meal ended, I excused myself, telling Gene I would meet him back at the sanctuary for the next service.

I searched for a quiet place. The Lord and I had to do some serious conversing. I went to the women's rest room, rushed into a stall, and locked the door behind me.

"OK, Lord," I piped up as if I was giving orders, "I'm tired of this runaround." Then I said the same words I had heard just a short time before, "I want You to show me before this next service is over whether I am lost or saved."

I still remember everything that happened after that. Gene and I returned to the evening service, but I did not have the slightest idea what the preacher was preaching because the Lord and I were having a conversation. It went something like this:

"OK, Lord, if I'm lost, why have I been able to lead so many people to accept You as Savior?"

"Virginia," He responded, "the Word of God and the Holy Spirit have brought them to Me. Not you."

"OK, Lord, if I'm lost, how did I know that Mary Lynn was lost?"

"Virginia, you have been around so many born-again Christians that you know how they should behave. You are observant and you could tell from her behavior that she did not exhibit characteristics of a Christian."

"OK, Lord, If I'm lost, why have you answered so many of my prayers?"

"Virginia, you have been praying according to My will. You have had the right motive in praying and I answered your prayers."

No more questions came to my mind. I sat there silent, pondering my condition.

Then a revelation came to me from the Lord. It was the Scripture passage of a king who prepared a wedding banquet for his son and called everyone to the banquet. None of those invited would come, so the king sent his servants out into the streets to gather all the people they could find to come to the banquet. One person entered the banquet not wearing wedding clothes. When the king saw him, he asked, "Friend, how did you get in here without wedding clothes?" The man was speechless. The king had him cast out into outer darkness.

Compassionately, the Lord declared to me, "Virginia, you are trying to get into heaven with your own robe of righteousness. Your righteousness is as filthy rags before Me. You must come to Me by the shed blood of My Son Jesus. If you do not, I will cast you into outer darkness, just like the king did with the wedding guest."

I had my answer. The Lord had revealed my sinful condition to me. He convinced me that I could never reach the holiness of God on my own. I had known for years that Jesus had died for my sins; but I had not acknowledged this fact with my heart, only my head. I had never understood it with my heart until that evening. The searchlight of the Holy Spirit had come to shine in on me, uncovering my own efforts, self-righteousness, and depravity.

I walked to the sanctuary altar and kneeled. Bowing my head, I asked Christ to come into my life.

I imagine the angels in heaven were standing on their tiptoes to hear my prayer that night. I prayed, "Lord, forgive me of my sinful condition. Forgive me for trying to live the Christian life in my own strength. I thank You for the blood that Jesus shed on the cross for my sins. I ask You now to take my sins and cast them as far as the east is from the west. Thank You that it will no longer be me trying to live the Christian life, but it will be You living through me. Amen."

As I lifted my head, I knew that Christ had done it all for me. He had wiped my sins away and His Holy Spirit had come to live inside me. Peace flooded my soul, and I felt a joy that was incomparable to anything I have ever felt.

At last I had my answer! At last I had peace! At last I had a relationship with Jesus! There is nothing comparable to Him, nothing more valuable.

Since that day in January 1975, Jesus has been with me through every event in life. Without knowing Jesus in that intimate way, I could not have survived the untimely death of my father to cancer at age 53. His death occurred just 2 years after my salvation experience. Without Christ, I could never have handled the spectacular addition of four children to our home. The wisdom I needed to raise those precious children during their teenaged years came only because Christ was at my side. And without Christ, I certainly could not have obeyed when the Lord instructed us to leave our family in Texas and moved to California first, and then to Illinois. Christ has given me the encouragement, endurance, and love that has been necessary to stay where He has placed us.

Discussion Starters

1. When and where did you come to know Christ as your personal Savior?

2. Did you have any problem understanding your need for repentance?

3. Was there a special person instrumental in leading you to Christ?

4. Were you raised in a Christian home?

5. In what ways has your life been different since you trusted in Christ?

4

Secure to Be You

God allowed me to find the real me through the study of His Word and prayer. As certain essentials became a part of my life, I didn't need to worry that I couldn't play the piano or sing a solo. God gave me the security to be myself. I didn't have any musical ability, but I did have lots of love for people.

Security Through Salvation

What is salvation? It's knowing Christ in a personal way. For a long time I had a head knowledge of Christ, but my knowledge stopped there. I loved the Lord with all my heart, served Him faithfully, prayed regularly, and received answers to my prayers. I read my Bible and tried to obey its commands. I was a minister's wife. But I found out there was more than this to being a Christian.

Some of you may be just like me. I was a Cornelius. Cornelius loved the Lord, prayed often, gave alms, and lived a good life. But it wasn't until Peter told him about Jesus that he truly was born again. (See Acts 10.)

If you have any doubts about your salvation, He will compassionately answer your prayers and show you. First John 1:9 (NIV) says, "If we confess our sins, he is faithful and just and will forgive us our sins and purify us from all unrighteousness."

God is faithful, and He will reveal Himself to you. God will strengthen you as you seek to know Him. Commit yourself to be like Jacob, who wrestled with the angel of the Lord all night long saying, "I will not let you go unless you bless me" (Gen. 32:25 NIV).

Secure in Christ's Love

We are like rare jewels to God. Nothing can replace us. In Isaiah 43:4 (NIV) God tells us, "Since you are precious and honored in my sight, and because I love you, I will give men in exchange for you, and people in exchange for your life." *Precious* means we are cherished, loved, guarded, and considered most valuable. God loves us as we are. He does not base His love for us on our performance. It is impossible to please all people all the time. Therefore, we need only to concentrate on pleasing the Lord. "And even the very hairs of your head are all numbered," says Matthew 10:30 (NIV). God's love for us is faithful and lasting throughout all eternity.

Get into the Word and meditate upon it regularly. As you read God's Word daily, ask Him to engrave on your heart the unconditional love that He has just for you.

Claim and memorize Scripture verses about God's love for you. Write Scripture verses on notecards and put them on your refrigerator, on the bathroom mirror, by the kitchen sink, at your computer, and in your car. Two good verses to begin with are 1 Peter 5:7 (NIV), "Cast all your anxiety on him because he cares for you"; and Jeremiah 29:11 (NIV), "'For I know the plans I have for you,' declares the Lord, 'plans to prosper you and not to harm you, plans to give you hope and a future.'" As you focus on the Word of God, you will dispel Satan's lies that seek to bring you down.

Reading Christian books is another way to grow in God's grace. Through the writings of others, we can grow in our knowledge of Him. *The Search for Significance* by Robert S.

McGee helped me to recognize that my significance comes from the Lord. I learned to dispel Satan's lies and exchange them for God's truth. It was such a liberating experience to discover that God loves me unconditionally, and I didn't need to worry about pleasing anyone except Him. When I discovered that I didn't need to fit into anyone's mold or stereotype, it freed me to be me!

Secure in a Call

Confident in the Lord, it seemed He quietly and softly called me into the ministry too. What a surprise! As I was helping Gene to fulfill his call in the ministry, God called me too! "Do two walk together unless they have agreed to do so?" (Amos 3:3 NIV). God never makes a mistake. I believe He puts a couple together who can complement one another. How brilliant our God is!

Many Scripture verses address a "call." Every person who has been born again by the Spirit of Christ has been called to serve Him in a manner that is worthy of Christ. This calling comes to all people, male and female. All are to trust our God and let God lead them where He takes them. Each of us originally trusted God for our salvation, and in like manner we must trust Him for our place of service as well. Ephesians 4:1–4,7 (NIV) tells us: "As a prisoner for the Lord, then, I urge you to live a life worthy of the calling you have received. Be completely humble and gentle; be patient, bearing with one another in love. Make every effort to keep the unity of the Spirit through the bond of peace. There is one body and one Spirit—just as you were called to one hope when you were called. . . . But to each one of us grace had been given as Christ apportioned it."

In Ephesians 4:1 we see the *dignity* of our call to serve God. We are to lead lives worthy of that high calling which comes from the Lord. In Ephesians 4:2–3 we recognize the *duty* of our call. Our duty in following the call from God is to live our lives as Christ did, with humility, gentleness, patience, and love. Ephesians 4:4 emphasizes that our call is *not to be divided.* There is one Christ, one Spirit, and one hope of our calling from God. Finally, Ephesians 4:7 explains the *discovery* of our call. God gives each one His grace according to the measure of giftedness He appoints to us. We must discover what gifts Christ has bestowed upon us and use those gifts in His service.

This calling from God is *secure* as we enter into the kingdom of God as His child. Romans 11:29 tells us that the gifts and calling of God are irrevocable. Second Timothy 1:8–9 (NIV) explains: "So do not be ashamed to testify about our Lord, or ashamed of me his prisoner. But join with me in suffering for the gospel, by the power of God, who has saved us and called us to a holy life—not because of anything we have done but because of his own purpose and grace. This grace was given us in Christ Jesus before the beginning of time."

If you are a child of God, then God has called you to serve Him in a special way. If you are married to a minister, then God has called you to serve beside your husband for the glory of God. You are not called to self-sufficiency, but rather to dependence on God. You are not called to duplicate or imitate the work of your husband. You are called to use your unique gifts alongside your husband. You are just as important as your husband and you are just as called. God has saved you, called you, and equipped you for His service. Your service will be different from your husband's service, but it is just as significant!

When I was just beginning in ministry alongside my husband, the Scriptures about being called burned like candles deep in my soul. Their flames grew brighter with each passing day. They comforted me with the knowledge that it was God Who had called me, and it would be God Who performed the work in me. First Thessalonians 5:24 (NIV) promises, "The one who calls you is faithful and he will do it." Isaiah 41:9–10 (NIV) affirms, "'You are my servant'; I have chosen you and have not rejected you. So do not fear, for I am with you; do not be dismayed, for I am your God. I will strengthen you and help you; I will uphold you with my righteous right hand."

Discussion Starters

1. In what three ways can you be secure to be you? Do you have these securities in your life?

2. What are several things that you can do to assure yourself of God's love?

3. Using Ephesians 4, explain the "call of the Lord."

4. Do you believe that everyone is "called" into service for the Lord? What Scripture verses emphasize this?

5. What does 1 Thessalonians 5:24 mean to you?

5

Principles for Finding Your Gifts

The moment you received Christ as your personal Savior, the Holy Spirit came to live inside you. With the residence of the Holy Spirit came gifts. These gifts were given to you to be used in the body of Christ. The Lord chooses what gifts He will give you; it is not your choice. He wants you to use these gifts to give Him glory.

Have you ever heard a kitten bark or a cow oink? That's ridiculous, you say! You are absolutely right! And it is just as ridiculous for us to try to act like someone else. Just as no two snowflakes are alike, so are there no two ministers' wives alike. God has made us just the way He wants us.

So why do we try to copy others? To be a carbon copy is the path of least resistance. But with just a little digging, you can uncover the gifts that God has given you. Your gifts suit your personality and temperament better than anyone else. You can be you better than anyone else!

First Principle: Don't Imitate Others

One sunny morning, Kathy, wife of a minister of youth, was having coffee with her best friend, Laura, wife of a minister of music in another local church. While laughing, talking, and watching Kathy's toddler, Ryan, play on the kitchen floor, the phone rang. It was Tim, Kathy's husband. Kathy's face glowed with delight as Tim relayed a message to her.

When Kathy hung up the phone, she gleefully reported to Laura, "Well, we have been officially called to come to a church in San Antonio. Tim was just notified by the search committee. They want us to be there in two months. I'm so excited about the church. The people are friendly and loving and the community is beautiful. I know our whole family will be happy there."

"Oh, Kathy," replied Laura, "I'm so thrilled for you. I've heard so many great things about that church. But doesn't it intimidate you a little to try to live up to the reputation of the former minister of youth's wife?"

"I don't know what you mean, Laura," said Kathy. "I really don't know anything about her."

"You're kidding," she said. "I thought everyone knew about her. She is 'Mrs. Organization.' She has more talent in her little finger than most persons do in their entire bodies. She organized and led a large youth drama group. She's known for her great personality and her ability to train the youth group in acting!"

As Kathy listened to the glowing account of the former minister of youth's wife, she couldn't help but notice the chipped polish on her nails and the smudges on her windows.

In an attempt to reassure herself, Kathy replied, "I'm sure everything will work out fine, Laura. After all, no one should expect me to be like someone else. I'm my own person."

Raising an eyebrow in doubt, Laura jumped up. "Well, got to run. We're really happy for you. All I can say is I'm glad it's you and not me. See you tomorrow."

Out the door she charged, "Mrs. Encouragement." *With friends like that, who needs enemies?* thought Kathy. *How am I going to measure up to "Mrs. Organization" with her many talents and glowing personality? There is nothing spectacular about me.*

Grabbing Ryan in one arm and a bottle of juice in the other, Kathy settled in her rocking chair. There she and the

Lord conversed while she rocked Ryan to sleep. Beside the rocking chair was her well-worn Bible still open to the passage she had studied just that morning. After rocking Ryan to sleep and putting him to bed, she returned to the passage in 1 Corinthians 12:1,8–11 (NIV): "Now about spiritual gifts, brothers, I do not want you to be ignorant. . . . There are different kinds of gifts, but the same Spirit. There are different kinds of service, but the same Lord. There are different kinds of working, but the same God works all of them in all men. Now to each one the manifestation of the Spirit is given for the common good. To one there is given through the Spirit the message of wisdom, to another the message of knowledge by means of the same Spirit, to another faith by the same Spirit, to another gifts of healing by that one Spirit, to another miraculous powers, to another prophecy, to another the ability to distinguish between spirits, to another the ability to speak in different kinds of tongues, and to still another the interpretation of tongues. All these are the work of one and the same Spirit, and he gives them to each man, just as he determines."

As Kathy meditated on these Scriptures, she prayed, "Lord, I don't have the gift of organization, and I've never been accused of having it all together, but I do love people. Lord, You have shown me what my gifts are. I know that I have the gifts of helps, teaching, and mercy. Please use these gifts in the new church for Your glory. Help me not to try to be like anyone else, especially the former minister of youth's wife. I promise to rely on You, Lord, if You will let these gifts shine through me. Amen."

Just like Kathy, the moment you received Christ as your Savior gifts were given you. God gave you these gifts so that (1) you would be useful in the church, the body of Christ; (2) the body of Christ would be made complete; and (3) the kingdom of God might be extended for God's glory.

In his book, *Your Spiritual Gifts Can Help Your Church Grow,* C. Peter Wagner explains how God intended for spiritual gifts to enhance the growth of the church and give glory to Him. In order to recognize your gifts you need to know what gifts there are. Gifts include prophecy, service, teaching, exhortation, giving, leadership, mercy, knowledge, faith, discernment, apostleship, administration, evangelism, shepherding, hospitality, intercession, and music.

Discovery of your spiritual gifts is not always easy. If you are not sure of your gifts, ask the Holy Spirit to reveal them to you and study God's Word. The following Scriptures address spiritual gifts: 1 Corinthians 12:8–10, Romans 12:6–8, Ephesians 4:11, and 1 Peter 4:10–11. Keep in mind James 1:5 (NIV): "If any of you lacks wisdom, he should ask God, who gives generously to all without finding fault." The Lord wants you to know and use your spiritual gifts. Spiritual gifts tests abound. Find one to help you discern your gifts. Or, use the following four techniques to determine your spiritual gifts.

1. Accept that God has given you, at salvation, spiritual gifts. Know that God wants you to use these gifts for the furtherance of His kingdom. God is the provider of these gifts, and all that God gives is good.

2. Prayerfully study passages in the Bible that explain spiritual gifts. Ask the Holy Spirit to reveal your gifts.

3. Make a detailed list of activities you enjoy doing. The activities you enjoy doing will usually reveal a particular gift or gifts that God has given you in order to accomplish those tasks successfully.

4. Ask God to lead you into a work or service in the church which will utilize your gifts. Second Timothy 1:6 (KJV) says, "Stir up the gift of God, which is in you."

Two important rules will always hold true concerning spiritual gifts: (1) the gift will be something that you enjoy; (2) the gift will be something others enjoy you doing. Wonderful, isn't it, how God made it that way!

Ministers and ministers' wives need to remember a spiritually elite group does not exist to do the work in the body of Christ. All people in the body are gifted, and all are important for the proper functioning of the body. Therefore, a minister or his wife is not anymore gifted or important than any other member in the church. All born-again members are to work together to make the body complete, all using their gifts.

In the past, churches have committed a grave error by allowing congregations to think that God has called and gifted only ministers in His service. Nothing could be further from the truth or New Testament teachings. The New Testament teaches that the combined gifts from all persons in the body are needed to make the body complete. Romans 12:4–6 (NIV) states, "Just as each of us has one body with many members, and these members do not all have the same function, so in Christ we who are many form one body, and each member belongs to all the others. We have different gifts, according to the grace given us."

Because of this erroneous idea that only the minister and his wife are gifted, many a minister and his wife have suffered from burnout, trying unsuccessfully to accomplish all jobs in the church. At the same time, church members sit in the pews bored and feeling useless. When this occurs in a church, the church will quit growing and become stagnant because it is not functioning according to God's plan.

Getting back to Kathy. During her first year in San Antonio, no one said anything to Kathy about the former minister of youth's wife. One day a friend shared with her, "Kathy, it is so refreshing to have a minister of youth's wife who loves young people the way you do. It's great to see you using your gifts to lift up our young people. They appreciate you so much because you show personal attention to each one."

With that statement, Kathy prayed silently, *Thank You, Lord, for Your faithfulness.* She remembered the prayer she had offered up to God to use her gifts for His glory in this new place of service. The church appreciated Kathy because she used her own gifts and didn't try to imitate someone else.

Second Principle: Learn to Say No

The greatest advice I ever received as a new minister's wife was learn to say no! *No* is a liberating word. Attempting to be all things to all people produces burnout. If you are not gifted in an area or you don't have the time, say no.

Soon after Gene began pastoring, I had to admit I did not have the gift of helps. But we had many women in our church who did. They could quickly and efficiently organize ministry in a time of illness or death. Not me. After several feeble attempts, I followed my own advice and said no. I let the women who were gifted in this area handle it. They were happy and so was I.

No stars will be added to your crown for stealing another person's opportunity to use her gifts in the church. Use discernment in accepting positions people want to give you. Avoid frustration. Serve in the areas of your giftedness.

Third Principle: Know Your Limitations

"Virginia, wake up. It's time to go home." I awoke to find John, our minister of youth, shaking me gently. "Are you all right?" he asked. "You look a little sick!"

I sat up in my bedroll and rubbed my swollen eyes, I couldn't believe I had slept through yet another youth lock-in. These all-night lock-ins were real torture for me. Feeling like I was going to throw up, I shook my heavy head. "I really did want to stay up for the talent show!" I exclaimed.

"Don't worry about it, Virginia. You just need to go home and get some rest. You look a little green around the gills."

My head pounding and my body aching, I retorted, "I just wish I could be of more use at these lock-ins. I always seem to cave in long before anyone else!"

"Virginia, let's face it. This just isn't your thing," commented John. "Right now you need to get home and get some sleep so you will be worth something tomorrow." I had to admit that my body demands more rest than most folks.

All of us have our own limitations. Even Einstein couldn't tie his shoes as a boy and was nearly thrown out of school. None of us, no matter how gifted or intelligent, can do everything well. If not readily accepted, your limitations can be a deterrent to understanding the real you.

Admit your limitations. Others will find out soon enough anyway. It's good for church members to know you are human just like they are. Dispel the myths that ministers' wives are supersaints. Let others know you get tired, cry, feel lonely, and have bad days! Don't let others put you on a pedestal. If you do, the only way to go is down! Lose that halo, but keep the wings. When you do, you'll enjoy life more and build deeper relationships with others.

Fourth Principle: Know the Word of God

Nothing can give a minister's wife more confidence and joy than knowing and obeying the Word of God. Knowing the Word of God will keep you focused on the Lord and keep you sane in this sometimes insane world. Know what you believe and why you believe it. Be grounded in the Word doctrinally so that you are not misled or confused.

Too much importance today is placed on feelings and experiences. Too little is said about studying the Word of God. The Word of God is our standard, our guide. Different philosophies, ideas, and trends will come and go; but the Word of God will remain forever.

Studying the Word of God regularly helps us grow in wisdom. Through the good and bad of life, the knowledge of the Word keeps us grounded in the Lord. The wisdom of the Word will produce leadership qualities and success in our lives.

God's Word also has a transforming ability as we study and apply it to our lives. In addition, knowing the Word of God enables us to pray according to God's will.

In America we are bombarded by Satan with messages contrary to God's Word. He targets our minds and emotions, substituting the world's standards for God's standards.

As you study God's Word, you will learn of the value you have as a woman—the beautiful woman God intends you to be. This kind of woman is not like any woman you see on television, with perfect hair, perfect body, perfect clothes. This woman is a woman of purity, love, loyalty, good works, dignity, kindness, and wisdom. Consistently apply 2 Timothy 2:15 and 2 Timothy 3:16–17 (NIV): "Do your best to present yourself to God as one approved, a workman who does not need to be ashamed and who correctly handles the word of truth. . . . All Scripture is God-breathed and is useful for teaching, rebuking, correcting and training in righteousness, so that the man of God may be thoroughly equipped for every good work."

Discussion Starters
1. What are the four principles for finding your gifts?

2. Do you know your spiritual gifts? Have you ever taken a spiritual gifts test? How have you been using your gifts in the church?

3. Have you ever tried to imitate the spiritual gifts of another person in the church? Have you ever served in the ministry in an area in which you were not gifted? What were the results?

4. Do you know your limitations? How do you try to avoid these areas?

5. How do you approach making decisions, such as where to serve and what to do?

6

Personality Secrets

Virginia, we've been invited to the Simpsons' home Thursday night for dinner. We need to leave about 6:00," relayed my hurried husband as he raced to the door one morning, briefcase in hand.

"But, Gene, I'm tired of being around people," I wailed. "I'm with young people all day long at school, and we've spent two nights at the church this week already. I love the Simpsons, but I just want to spend a quiet night at home."

"Virginia," he answered, "I'm with people all day long too, but it doesn't bother me. What's wrong with you? Don't you like people?"

"Of course I do," I retorted. "But after awhile all I want to do is go to my room, snuggle up with a good book, and be by myself. After being with 150 young people all day at school, I don't want to talk to anyone when I get home. I don't know why I feel that way. I just do!"

Gene and I have had this conversation in every place we have lived. The names and places have changed, but the topic has stayed the same. It seemed there was always another engagement to attend, another dinner to host. Yet I was tired of being around people. Gene and I could never agree on our social calendar.

Finally, our dilemma was identified when we took a test

which categorizes persons according to temperament. Gene and I had the opportunity to take the Myers-Briggs Type Indicator. Based on a theory of types and temperaments, this test measures four sets of preferences, or types. Each set is a pair of opposite traits. Persons are "typed" according to where they fall in between the pairs of opposite traits. The four pairs of opposites are extroversion-introversion, sensing-intuitive, feeling-thinking, and judging-perceiving.

From the Myers-Briggs inventory, I found out why we could not agree on a social calendar. I am an introvert. Gene is an extrovert. I discovered that introverts can love people just as much as extroverts, but introverts and extroverts receive their energy in opposite ways. An extrovert thrives on being with people. People pump her up and give energy back to her. An introvert, on the other hand, enjoys being with people, but people deplete her of energy. The more she is with people, the more she uses energy. When her energy is used up, she must take time to be by herself in order to get recharged. That quiet, alone time is essential for an introvert.

When Gene and I discovered we were opposites on this aspect of our personalities, we understood why we always disagreed on church activities. Gene learned I really did need to be home by myself at times so that I could get refreshed and recharged for the next meeting or social event. After Gene realized that it was essential to my personality, he began to encourage me to stay home at times for my own welfare. After I received the energy I needed from being alone, I was ready to enjoy another social function with enthusiasm.

The book *Type Talk at Work* by Otto Kroeger and Janet Thuesen explains type and temperament theory in greater detail. A whole new world will open up to you as you begin to understand how God put together your particular personality. No one personality type is better than another; all are significant. The Myers-Briggs Type Indicator identifies 16 different personality combinations. In each combination are strengths and weaknesses.

Read books available on the topic to help you understand personality and how it affects our behavior. Through reading books and attending seminars, Gene and I have gained new skills in understanding each other's personalities and meeting each other's needs.

Often the Lord causes opposites to be attracted to one another and marry. Each mate can help the other in his or her areas of weakness. We need to look beyond ourselves and our ways of doing things to consider the needs and desires of our mates. In doing so, we become more well-rounded and stronger persons.

The Case of a Shy Shannon

Gene and I were being introduced as the new minister and his wife at North Central Church. The long receiving line of people trailed off into oblivion as members waited patiently to greet us. I had shaken several dozen hands when I began to feel my stomach rumble. Suddenly, I could take no more. I dashed out to locate the nearest rest room. Every eye in the room turned to watch me as I ran. What a way to start off our new pastorate! I was sick again! Why couldn't I handle this? Every time I got nervous, I became violently ill.

Being shy and being a minister's wife mix together about as well as oil and water. Yet you would probably be amazed at how many ministers' wives are shy by nature. It is a painful position to be in. I know because I have relived the previous story more times than I care to admit.

As I said earlier, Gene is an extrovert by nature. He never meets a stranger and never lacks for something to say. Gene has a booming, vibrant voice that easily projects across a room. I, on the other hand, have a soft, quiet voice that no one can hear. I so wanted to be like Gene when we were first married; but I soon gave up, realizing it was impossible.

Ever since I was young, just the thought of walking into a room full of people turned me into gelatin. I was petrified! I would shiver and shake, trying to figure out what to say. My immediate response was always to turn on my heels and run.

Sometimes my bashfulness was misconstrued as conceit.

Words of wisdom in overcoming shyness are found in 1 Corinthians 5:17 (KJV): "Therefore, if any man be in Christ, he is a new creature: old things are passed away; behold, all things are become new." From that verse I learned God could help me to be whatever He wanted me to be. Even though I was born with a shy nature, God could make new things happen in my life. When I realized this truth, I began claiming the verse for my shyness. The Lord did not want me to feel inadequate or intimidated by others. Therefore, His Spirit began giving me confidence and assurance when I was around people. It has been a slow, but beautiful, transformation.

Second Timothy l:7 (KJV) says, "For God hath not given us the spirit of fear; but of power, and of love, and of a sound mind." For years I thought this Scripture was for everyone else but me! But the more I fed on the Word of God, the more I came to believe that "with God all things are possible!" (Matt. 19:26 NIV).

Psalm 37:4 (NIV) tells us, "Delight yourself in the Lord and he will give you the desires of your heart." I had been praying for boldness. In answer, God put me in a situation that forced me to develop it. I became a ninth-grade English teacher.

My job was to prepare 150 adolescents for high school. It was a lot like being an army drill sergeant. My instructions had to be clear and concise, easily understood, and repeated over and over.

Now, whoever heard of a quiet, shy drill instructor? I learned I had to either take charge and run the class, or be run over by the class. God certainly tried me with fire! I had no choice but to learn to raise my voice and speak sternly. I quickly learned how to speak and act with authority. I might have been shy, but I wasn't stupid.

More than any other activity in my life, teaching ninth-graders helped me overcome my shyness. I had no choice. It was either overcome or be overcome. Isn't it amazing how the Lord puts us in situations that enable us to be what He knows we can be?

Now, when I find myself in a room full of people, I begin asking questions. I ask the person next to me to tell me about himself or herself. To get conversation flowing, I use starters such as these:

•Tell me about your work.
•Tell me about your family.
•Tell me about your home.
•Tell me about what you have been doing lately.
•Tell me about your hobbies.
•Tell me about your grandchildren.

These statements are foolproof because everyone likes to talk about himself or herself! Just pay attention as the person talks; smile and make comments when appropriate. When the person finishes talking, he or she will think you are a great conversationalist because you listened. People just want to know that you are interested in them.

Giving Speeches

Ministers' wives are often called upon to give speeches. This can be a terrifying experience for a bashful person. Here are some hints to remember in preparing a speech: (1) prepare your speech thoroughly; (2) sprinkle in humor as much as you can; (3) consider your audience; (4) relax and have fun.

Ninety-five percent of the success of your delivery is determined by your body language, voice intonation, and general attitude. As remarkable as it may seem, when giving a presentation only 7 percent is communicated by the words; 38 percent is communicated by tone of voice; and 55 percent is communicated by facial and body language. The audience sums up your message in the first two minutes of your presentation. So, make your introduction exciting and relevant to your audience. Smile, use enthusiastic body language, look at them, and enjoy yourself.

Consider ahead of time who your audience is and what they want to learn from you. Try to get them actively involved in some way. People would much rather participate than listen passively. Use visual aids and kinesthetic activities when possible. Try to get your audience as excited about your topic as you are by using personal anecdotes, humor, and interesting stories along the way.

After years of trusting the Lord to help me overcome my shyness, people are astounded now to learn I am an introvert. I'm not scared of crowds anymore. I really do enjoy meeting and getting to know people now.

The Case of a Mouthy Martha

If you are an extrovert, the previous information does not apply to you. However, from the experiences of my extrovert friends, I know that you have to be concerned with saying too much. As the wife of a minister, you are privy to information that could cause hurt to others. You must guard what you say to well-meaning friends who want to know everything that is going on.

The same principle of dependence upon the Lord holds true for an extrovert as well. God can help refine that copious nature of yours to bring glory to Him. Spend time every day in His Word. Pray, memorize specific Scriptures about speaking with wisdom, and ask for God's help. As you depend on God and His Word, He will fill your mouth with just the right words. He will show you how to keep your mouth shut at just the right times.

It may be you are an extrovert and your husband is an introvert. You may be tempted to speak for your husband when he does not answer quickly in conversation. You may need to take a deep breath and silently count to ten when someone asks your husband a question in your presence.

Once again, pray for the situation and ask the Lord to help you be sensitive to your husband's needs and responses. As you rely on the Lord to speak with wisdom, He will amaze you with the discretion He gives you. Others will begin to consider you a wise person, instead of a talkative one.

Discussion Starters

1. Have you and/or your husband taken the Myers-Briggs Type Indicator? What is your type? What is your husband's type?

2. How do these types affect how you serve the Lord?

3. Do you suffer from shyness? Have you been able to overcome your shyness? How were you able to do so? What Scriptures helped you with shyness?

4. Have you had experiences of a Mouthy Martha? How have you been able to blend your extrovert nature with your husband's nature? What Scriptures helped you?

5. What personality-related issues have you encountered in being a minister's wife? How did you resolve these issues?

Part 2

Understanding
and
Appreciating
Your Mate

7

Reeds of Every Woman

We have all seen the couple that sits at the dinner table in a restaurant looking lonely and bored with each other. They say very few words and they never touch. They both look like they wish they were somewhere else. Was this the same couple that talked eagerly with each other when they dated? They were so much in love! What happened?

Something changed after the wedding. After years of responsibilities and pressures, they don't know how to make each other happy anymore. They don't understand the needs of the other and his or her own needs are not being met.

Add to this the responsibilities of working on a church staff or other ministry staff and the pressures of trying to meet the needs of all the people who need your help and you have huge problems. On top of this, many people seem to expect the minister and his wife to have a perfect relationship. With all these pressures, you often have a couple who is on the brink of breakup rather than the perfect relationship. How can you avoid this?

Several things must be done to avoid this sad scenario. First, you must learn that you can never meet all the needs of the people who come seeking your help. Second, it is unrealistic to think you can fulfill all the expectations of the people to whom you and your husband minister. When you fulfill God's expectations for you and demonstrate a Christ-like love, that is enough. Third, learn what your needs are and what your husband's needs are. Understanding how God made men and women different emotionally and socially is just as important as learning about our differences sexually. Let's start with your needs first.

Every woman has four basic needs: affection, meaningful conversation, openness and honesty, and security. These needs stay with you no matter what you do or how old you are. These needs are opposite from a man's needs, and it is up to you to lovingly talk with your husband about these needs. In doing so, you must talk about his needs and how to meet them.

Affection

According to Willard Harley Jr. in *His Needs, Her Needs,* the first basic need for every woman is affection. This affection includes hugs, kisses, and holding hands. It reflects any kind of thoughtfulness, tenderness, and gentleness that does not have to do with sex. Women enjoy sex only after receiving large doses of tender affection. Men don't have the same need. You must talk with your husband about your need for affection. You have to communicate your desires.

Explain that through such thoughtful things as calling you during the day, opening the door for you, holding your hand, complimenting you, doing the dishes, or helping with the children, he is actually helping you to prepare for love-making later. Acknowledge his gentle acts of affection. Let him know that little acts of kindness mean a lot to you.

Never take your husband's thoughtfulness for granted. Make sure he knows you appreciate his tenderness. Don't get angry because you think he should automatically know what to do to meet your needs. Does your husband look forward to seeing you at the end of a day? Be attractive, be sweet, be funny. Always remember, a man does think differently from a woman because he has different needs.

John Gray's book *Men Are from Mars, Women Are from Venus* explains this phenomenon. Gray emphasizes that men and women speak a different language. Women don't say what they mean. They expect men to "figure out" what they mean by dropping hints. The problem is men don't understand hints. Hints don't compute. Men understand black-and-white, concrete statements.

Let me give you an example. When a wife is angry at her husband about something and he asks her what is wrong, she may say, "Oh, nothing! Just go away and leave me alone!" When a man hears that, he thinks his wife wants him "to go away and leave her alone" because that is what she just told him. He is a concrete thinker. However, we know that this is not what a woman means at all. She may have said that, but what she really means is, "I want you to gently put your arms around me and give me a hug. Tell me that you care about me and my feelings." Do you see what I mean? We women do not say what we mean; but, we expect our husbands to read our minds. No one can do that. We need to be more specific and honest about our needs. Don't use innuendos or hints. Tell him you need a hug, a kiss. Take his hand when you want to hold hands. Tell him in very clear language exactly what you need.

When he sends you flowers or hands you a gift, acknowledge your appreciation with a tender phone call or a big hug and kiss when he walks in the door. Be careful not to criticize the cost or that the flowers aren't your favorite color. Most men have fragile egos and criticism can be devastating.

A husband receives pleasure in seeing his wife happy. The trouble is some women don't know how to show happiness. If you want your husband to know how to treat you, you must learn how to express joy when he surprises you. Your husband will be drawn to this type of enthusiasm and sensitivity. Give it to him and you will get it from him—thoughtfulness and affection, that is.

The two things that a man can't handle from his wife are anger and rejection. He doesn't know what to do with them.

If he gets anger and rejection too much, he will retreat. Eventually, he may retreat to another woman. Don't take that chance!

Meaningful Conversation

The second basic need for every woman is to have meaningful conversation with her husband. Girls come into this world talking more and talking faster than boys. Women crave the closeness that comes from meaningful conversation. A woman has a tremendous need for a man to share his goals, dreams, and aspirations with her. She wants to talk with him about her dreams and ambitions too. A man does not have a need for this type of conversation. Therefore, it's up to you to initiate meaningful conversation with your husband. You have to let him know how much dialogue means to you and how much you value what he has to say. In order to do this, refrain from criticism, bitterness, or put downs. Listen closely when he speaks. Let him know how special he is and how great you think he is. As you sincerely offer these compliments, he will begin to enjoy conversation with you and you with him.

Let your husband take his time when talking. Don't rush him and don't do all the talking. I still have to be careful not to talk too much with Gene because in doing so I sometimes stifle an idea or a thought he is trying to share. Often if you ask your husband to talk with you for a short amount of time, say 10 minutes, it encourages him because he will have a specific time boundary. When the 10 minutes of conversation are up, smile, give him a big hug, and tell him how much the conversation meant to you. This will encourage him towards longer conversations.

Openness and Honesty

The third basic need of every woman is for her husband to be honest and open with her. This goes right along with her need for conversation. As you are open and honest with your husband, it encourages him to do so with you. As a minister, let's hope that your husband is honest. If he is not, the only thing you can do is pray that God will work in his life in this area.

Openness in a man does not come naturally. He must be confident that he can trust you. A minister has to keep many confidences in his work. It is imperative that you not divulge any confidences to anyone. There are two absolutes in developing openness in your husband. You must never laugh at his ideas and you must never put him down for any reason. These two things will affect your husband's ego to the point that he may never share with you again.

Openness means being honest about feelings, being candid about successes and failures, and that leaves a spouse vulnerable. In Psalms it says that a wise woman builds her home, but a foolish woman tears it down. If you are not careful about openness, the confidences that have been entrusted to you can be broken and trust shattered. Apologies are difficult and often a problem for a man. Many men believe apologies make them look small in a woman's eyes. They do not realize that apologies have the opposite effect on a woman. It is up to you to communicate to your husband how you feel about apologies. Explain that when apologies are made, they show how much inner strength there is in your relationship and that talking about mistakes or failures honestly can restore openness. Once your husband understands how you feel about apologies, they should come easier.

Security

The fourth basic need of every woman is to have security in her relationship and financially. No matter how career-oriented a woman may be, she still wants to know that her husband has the ability to support her if necessary. If he cannot support her in the beginning, she will usually do everything she can to help him get the necessary education or training so he will be able to support her and the family in the future. A woman needs stability she can depend on emotionally and financially. It isn't easy being a minister's wife, a mother, a church worker, and an employee, but for many ministers' families it is necessary. Some women work because they enjoy their careers and receive fulfillment from them; however, this basic need is there. No matter what the ministry circumstances or the economic times are like, a woman needs to feel secure.

All of these needs (affection, conversation, honesty, and security) are important in a woman's life. If any one of these needs is ignored, problems will develop. The woman who has learned her own needs and knows how to translate those needs to her husband so that he can fulfill them is a wise and happy woman. The woman who has not learned this is usually frustrated and causes frustration for those around her.

I must insert here that no man can make a woman completely happy. Only God can do that as we rest in Him for all our needs. Philippians 4:19 (NIV) says, "And my God will meet all your needs according to his glorious riches in Christ Jesus." When you have tried to explain your needs to your husband and he doesn't get it, give it to God. Ask for God's help and demonstrate "a gentle and quiet spirit" as mentioned in 1 Peter 3. Let God do the rest.

Bragging on Brad

Beth is a beautiful niece of ours. Brad is Beth's husband and a terrific role model as a husband and father. Beth and Brad graciously open their home to family and friends alike. Gene and I are constantly making trips back to Texas. On several occasions, Beth and Brad have invited me to stay in their home. Brad is a successful lawyer and also very active in their church. However, he is never too busy to love his wife and care for their children. Many a time when we have visited in their home unexpectedly, we have observed Brad cleaning the kitchen after their evening meal while Beth tends to the children. He is perfectly comfortable with washing the dishes, cleaning off the table, and sweeping the floor.

At the end of a busy Sunday, everyone came home from church exhausted. It was Brad's custom to take the children up to bed by himself every Sunday evening to give Beth a break. Brad gently tucked each child in his or her bed, spoke softly to them of his love, and quietly said good night. What a wonderful way for the children to see their father's love. What a sweet way for a husband to tell his wife that he honors and treasures her!

If your husband is not meeting the basic needs in your life, make it a matter of prayer. Ask God to show you how to communicate with your husband. Pray that you will be the Christian wife he needs and that God will give you guidance as you talk with your husband. Be prayerful, loving, and patient as you nurture a love-filled relationship where your needs as well as his are understood and met.

Please remember, don't expect your husband to be perfect in meeting all your needs. That is impossible, just as it is impossible to meet all of his basic needs all the time. When your husband fails you or you fail him, focus on the Lord. God can give you what you need in life.

Discussion Starters

1. Name the first basic need of every woman. How can you tenderly talk with your husband to fulfill this need?
2. Name the second basic need of every woman. How can you communicate with your husband about fulfilling this need?
3. Name the third basic need of every woman. What are some creative ways to lovingly dialogue with your husband to fulfill this need?
4. Name the fourth basic need of every woman. Have you assisted your husband in fulfilling this need for you? How?
5. Does your husband have trouble apologizing? Do you do all the apologizing? Have you told your husband what you understand an apology to mean; and when a sincere apology is given, that healing comes in a relationship?

8

Needs of Every Man

Ephesians 5:21–26,28 (NASB) says, "And be subject to one another in the fear of Christ. Wives, be subject to your own husbands, as to the Lord. For the husband is the head of the wife, as Christ also is the head of the church, He himself being the Savior of the body. But as the church is subject to Christ, so also the wives ought to be to their husbands in everything. Husbands, love your wives, just as Christ also loved the church and gave Himself up for her. . . . So husbands ought also to love their own wives as their own bodies. He who loves his own wife loves himself."

God first created Adam and then Eve. She was taken from the side of Adam, from his rib. She was to be the help-mate suitable for Adam. God created Eve from Adam's side symbolizing the partnership of marriage. She was not created from the head to dominate nor was she created from the foot to be trodden underfoot, but from the side of man symbolizing that man and woman are to walk through life side by side.

It was always God's intention that husband and wife make a beautiful union in marriage. The husband and the wife are equally important. The husband is to love his wife as Christ loved the church. Christ never stood as an authoritarian demanding requests. Christ was never selfish, looking after His own needs. Christ always gave, always loved, and always forgave. Christ gave His very life for the church. Our husbands are to love us so much that they would be willing to give their lives for us. They are to honor, cherish, appreciate, and protect us. When we see Christlike love demonstrated, it is easy to return that love.

Sexual Fulfillment

In order for a woman to be suitable for her mate, she needs to know his basic needs. There are five of them. The first basic need for every man is sexual fulfillment. A strange phenomenon for a woman is that her husband does not need affection like she does. Many women, even those who have been married for years, do not realize this. A man does not need affection in order to experience sexual fulfillment. The question is: How do you receive the affection you need and how do you give the sexual fulfillment he needs? The answer is simple. You learn together. As you learn how to give the sexual fulfillment he needs, he learns how to give you affection. This learning process may take years, but it will be well worth it.

Touch is an important part of affection. When looking for furniture for our den, I explained to Gene that I would like a couch that we could both sit on when watching television rather than the usual two separate lounge chairs. I told him how much it would mean to me if we could hold hands and snuggle while watching TV together. We shopped around and found just the right sofa. Now we sit together while enjoying our favorite TV programs. Just this small adjustment in our home has made me much more receptive to his needs. I think he's glad he bought that couch.

God created sex to be a beautiful, tender union between husband and wife alone. God intended for the sexual act to be engaged, enjoyed, and cherished only in the context of a total lifetime commitment to one person. When two people make this pledge to one another through marriage, sexual fulfillment becomes a deep, satisfying pleasure that grows as the years go by.

If you sense problems with sexual fulfillment in your relationship, try to determine the cause. There are many wonderful books on sexual fulfillment in the marriage relationship by Christian authors. Read as much as you can and become as wise as you can. There could be several problems that relate directly to your husband's position as a minister. Your husband may be in a state of exhaustion from overwork. Many ministers are. If this is the case, talk and pray about the matter of priorities. Then, agree together to set some priorities. The marriage relationship should always come before the ministry. This doesn't mean that your marriage comes before God. Of course not. But your marriage must always have priority above the ministry. This is often a difficult concept for ministers to understand. Many feel that if they don't do everything everyone wants done, then they are not serving effectively. Nothing could be further from the truth. Trying to do all the ministry tasks for everyone else was never God's plan for service. God intends for each of us to use our gifts. Some ministers still try to do it all, and that can only create exhaustion and frustration. Find some good books about how the church, the family of faith, was designed by God to grow as everyone in the church works together, each using his or her own gifts.

Because of the nature of our husbands' work, we must constantly be on the lookout for the ugly culprit called burnout. Try to make sure that your husband has an outlet of regular recreation. It is not a luxury, it is a necessity! A man's body requires exercise to let off steam, frustration, and stress. Gene used to go hunting with his good buddy Royce Binnion in Porter, Texas, and Larry Osborn in Crowley, Texas. He also enjoys golf.

Often he and I would drive up the street to the nearest golf course and hit a bucket of balls if he didn't have time for nine holes. After a stressful day, it is amazing how much just hitting those balls relaxed him. With every swing, a small amount of stress seemed to fly away with that ball. We then went home to eat a relaxed meal and sleep soundly that night. Recreation of some kind on a regular basis will do a world of good for you and your stressed-out mate. Try to recreate with him if you can. You'll be amazed how much fun it can be.

The busier a man is in his job, the more essential it is that he take off for a little trip at least once a quarter. Set up regular "getaway" plans. Go to a hotel or bed-and-breakfast every two or three months for a change of scenery. Relax, laugh, have fun, and do the things you both enjoy. Revive that spark you had when you dated. We will always remember the gracious woman in our church in Porter, Texas, who often gave us the key to her lakeside cabin. During our ministry in Porter, Gene directed four major building programs in our church and her cabin was a blessed respite during those hectic years.

Before your trip, spend a little time jotting down the characteristics and qualities that you love and appreciate about each other. Then, at the right time, pull out your lists and share them. Being complimented and genuinely appreciated by your mate is endearing. Share your dreams and hopes with one another.

Enlist your church family to help you make these getaway trips as easy as possible. Keep in close contact with families that your children enjoy. While raising our four children, I arranged for four different families to care for them while we took our getaways. It was a great break for them and a terrific help for us.

If priorities, burnout, or physical problems are not issues in your relationship, perhaps a close self-evaluation is necessary. Is there a lack of intimacy because he has been rejected by your indifference at times? Has unforgiveness or bitterness formed a wall around your heart? Through prayer and counsel, the Lord can help you see your problem and enable you to love your husband again. You might recognize that your exhaustion is a problem. If that is the case, try to do some serious rescheduling and get more rest. If possible, hire someone to help with the housework and try to transfer some of your obligations to others. Remember, you can't do it all; and if you are too exhausted to enjoy your husband, then something else needs to go.

Treat this area of your relationship with candor, but delicately; with openness, but intimately. Learning about and meeting the basic need of sexual fulfillment will provide intimacy and strength within your relationship. It will bond you when the world tries to pull you apart.

Recreational Companionship

The second basic need for every man is to have a recreational companion. This statement precludes the necessity of every man to enjoy some type of recreation. Because God made men to be physical creatures, men require more physical activity. This is the reason most men enjoy sports so much. This is a fact of life, and we might as well get used to it.

The sooner we understand the male psyche and adjust to it, the easier life will be. Complaining about it won't change it. Every man desires that his wife be his companion in the pursuit of his recreational enjoyment. It thrills a man to have his wife at his side, enjoying the things he enjoys. A man is in his ultimate element when his wife is beside him enjoying a sports or recreational event.

Recently Gene and I led a seminar in Alaska with ministers and their wives. The seminar was at night so we played during the day. One of Gene's dreams has been to fish for king salmon. So, I went king salmon fishing with him. We had to get up at 4:45 A.M. and dress in about six layers of clothing. We fished during the rain for about three hours and then fished in the cold for another five. I did a lot of praying while I sat there freezing and holding that pole; but I really had a terrific time, especially when I caught that 35-pound salmon. The point is, fishing for king salmon would not have been my choice of recreational activities; but because of my love for Gene, I went. Gene was so proud of me and my catch. All the way back to Illinois he was brag-

ging and showing pictures of the fish I caught. I was willing
to be his recreational companion and he loved it.

Find a sport or activity that you both enjoy and pursue it
together. Let your husband know that you will be happy to
accompany him as long as he will give you attention and
not treat you like one of the boys. Help him to understand
that he needs to be considerate of your needs while you are
enjoying your activity together. Gene was very careful to
give me the attention I needed on our fishing trips. When
we went halibut fishing, Gene sat by me and at different
times checked on me to make sure I was doing all right.
Halibut fishing requires fishing off the bottom of the ocean
with 3-pound weights. Gene helped me bring in that huge
rod and reel several times. When I had caught my limit, he
knew I needed to rest inside the boat. I even got to take a
little nap inside the cabin on our 90-minute drive back to
shore. Before we went back to our motel that evening, we
indulged in some frozen yogurt and strolled down the vil-
lage streets hand in hand looking in the little shops for gifts,
one of my favorite forms of recreation.

Keep trying until you find activities that you enjoy
together. Golf is my new adventure with my husband. Finding a recreation that we both enjoy has not come easy, but
we keep trying. Don't give up, and you will find that being
your husband's recreational companion will become far
more exhilarating every year of your marriage.

An Attractive Wife

Every man needs a wife he can be proud of, one he thinks is
beautiful. Women are God's beautiful creation; and as
recorded in Proverbs 31:10 (NASB): "An excellent wife,
. . . her worth is far above jewels." You may not look like
the latest model, but you can be fresh, glowing, stylish, and
a little mysterious.

Don't let your imperfections become excuses. Take pride
in your appearance. Does your husband tell you that you are

attractive? If he doesn't, find out why. Maybe he has forgotten how important a compliment can be, or maybe you need to make some changes. Because your husband is a minister, you are both in a more public position. Take pride in your appearance. Find a great hairstyle; flattering clothes; good makeup; and, most of all, a smile. You'll be glad you took time for yourself; and so will he.

Domestic Help

Many men need a little help with domestic needs. Some men need more help than others. Of course, a clean home, hot meals, and clean clothes are the basics.

Home management is no small task, and it is a shame that our society has frowned on the abilities of homemakers. Because so many women work outside the home today, keeping the home comfortable and pleasant, rather than focusing on a house that is immaculate, is necessary. Often the husband will need to help with the home management, especially if the wife works outside the home. I believe a mother should also enlist her children to help. Each child should have his or her own set of chores to learn responsibility and teamwork. Teach your boys, as well as your girls, how to clean, wash, iron, and cook. They will make much better husbands and wives. But when it comes down to it, the buck stops with Mom. No matter how liberated our society tells us to be, the home reflects the managing ability of the woman. The primary domestic need for a man is that his home runs smoothly and peacefully. Your home needs to be a haven of rest, relaxation, and laughter. It needs to be a refreshing place to get recharged from the harshness and harassment of the world.

Admiration

Because a man gets most of his identity from his work, he has a need to be recognized in that work. He needs to know that others appreciate what he does, especially his wife. You can see a man almost puff up with pride when someone compliments him on his achievements.

Admiration is an essential need. It has to do with manhood and self-esteem. Because of this need, a wife must find ways to learn about her husband's work and compliment him on his endeavors. Sometimes she is the only one who believes in him. Often her admiration and appreciation spur him on to have the confidence to do bigger and better things in life. This is an essential part of being a helpmate to our husbands. We need to encourage, admire, and believe in them.

Christ wants the wife to love her husband as she loves the Lord Himself. In fact, every wife who is walking close to her Lord will study His Word, follow His leadership, and draw from His wisdom the words of affirmation and encouragement her husband needs.

Having felt the comfort of God's love and the affirmation of His respect, we cannot help but show the same love and respect to the husband that the Lord has given us on this earth. It then becomes a beautiful privilege to obey our Lord's words.

Praise your mate for the hard work he does in providing for you and your family. Treat him with respect in public and especially in front of the children. Let him know that his ideas and plans are valuable. Show him consideration and laugh at his jokes.

The following are some specific ways to show appreciation to your husband. Rate yourself on how you treat your husband in each area: *E* for Excellent, *G* for Good, or *N* for Needs Improvement. If you are really brave, ask your husband to rate you on how you treat him; then compare your ratings. A healthy discussion should ensue.

___ 1. Often express appreciation and admiration for the work he does.

___ 2. Brag on his abilities in front of people.

___ 3. Support him in front of your children.

___ 4. Show concern for him as well as the children.

___ 5. Listen lovingly to his problems without always giving advice.

__ 6. Be understanding when he has to work late.

__ 7. Don't nag (nagging is anything said more than once).

__ 8. Don't try to manipulate him.

__ 9. Don't harp on his faults.

__ 10. Show excitement about his ideas.

__ 11. Support him when no one else will.

__ 12. Verbally express the faith you have in his future.

__ 13. Enjoy sports or other activities with him.

__ 14. Try to adjust your schedule to his.

__ 15. Surprise him with things he enjoys.

__ 16. Enjoy lovemaking and initiate it yourself sometimes.

__ 17. Take pride in your appearance.

__ 18. Prepare with love the things he likes to eat.

__ 19. Make your home a place of peace, serenity, and laughter.

__ 20. Give him space to think, play, or just act like a kid.

__ 21. Be fun to be with; plan adventuresome dates.

__ 22. Be positive about your marriage and your life together.

__ 23. Express tenderness and gentleness toward him.

__ 24. Pray for him daily.

__ 25. Express often that you love being his wife.

Be on Guard!

I believe that God wants the husband and wife to be equal in the marriage partnership. Satan is trying to break up Christian homes in our country today. If he can break up a Christian home, Satan has accomplished a real victory. According to James Dobson in *Love for a Lifetime,* we need to avoid several marriage killers. These marriage killers are:

1. Overcommitment and exhaustion
2. Excessive credit and conflict over money
3. Interference from in-laws
4. Low self-esteem and jealousy

5. Any kind of addiction (alcohol, drugs, food, pornography, gambling, shopping)
6. Business or church failure
7. Business or church success

Because of the nature of your husband's work, the first marriage killer alone is the most difficult one to overcome. Overcommitment and exhaustion are predominant problems for most ministers. Combine this with the last marriage killer, church success, and we often see ministers' families caught in the marriage killer trap. Be on guard when you sense that you and/or your husband are overcommitted to ministry. Overcommitment to programs and activities, as well as doing all the work that needs to be done instead of equipping others to help, will take all the joy out of ministry, your marriage relationship, and everything that is dear.

Marriage killers 2 through 6 are easy to understand. However, many cannot imagine how church success can destroy a marriage; but it can. When a ministry is growing, your husband becomes energized. He begins working long hours just to keep up. With success also comes pride; and if one is not careful, arrogance for what has been accomplished rather than what God has blessed. In time, overcommitment and exhaustion affect even the most successful ministers. It will wear out the body physically, emotionally, and spiritually. Help your husband see warning signs and keep your marriage alive.

Enlist Churches to Pray for You

There are several pearls of wisdom that you can adopt to help avoid marriage killers. The first pearl is to ask individuals or churches to be your intercessors in prayer. I advise ministers and their wives to enlist churches that do not know them personally to pray for them. This way you can feel free to open up and share personal prayer needs with them confidentially. There are many churches across this country that have prayer closets and intercessors that love to pray for the needs of others regularly. They would be thrilled to pray for a minister and his family. Some problems in life need more prayer than we can give them. The more people you have praying for you, the more strongholds of Satan can be broken down.

The second pearl of wisdom is to ask your church family to pray for you as a family. If your church will agree to pray for you during their morning devotionals and briefly at every meal, it is amazing how many prayers will be offered up for you and your family in one day, one week, and one month. C. Peter Wagner's book *Prayer Shield* explains the importance of having people pray for you and your family regularly. You can never have too many prayer warriors. As these groups pray for you, you will sense a vitality and strength in your marriage and service for the Lord that was not there before.

The third pearl of wisdom is accountability. More and more ministers are realizing the importance of an account-ability group. Your husband needs a male group and you need a female group. An accountability group is two or three close Christian friends outside your church whom you admire and trust. Try to meet once a week or twice a month. Sometimes a call during the week can take the place of meeting together if schedules conflict. Talk with each other about your quiet time with the Lord, your marriage relation-ship, and the goals you have in your life. We all need to be held accountable, especially ministers and their wives. Accountability helps keep us on the right path and enables a closer walk with our Lord.

The fourth pearl of wisdom is to be open to professional, Christian counseling if necessary. Because your minister husband does so much counseling with others, it is often difficult to admit that counseling is necessary. But if there is serious depression, forced termination, or addiction of any kind, counseling may be necessary. Pray about the right counselor, and the Lord will give you direction. Often more than prayer is necessary to enable a minister or his wife to deal with problems.

Discussion Starters

1. What are the first three needs of every man? How are you helping to fulfill those needs?

2. Name the other two needs of every man. How specifically are you helping to fulfill those needs for your husband?

3. What are the seven marriage killers to watch out for in every marriage? How much time are you and your husband spending each week in recreation and conversation together?

4. What or where are some terrific getaways for you and your husband? Can you try to get away more often? Can you enlist some people in your church to help you with this project?

5. Do you and your husband have a group or groups that regularly pray for you? Do each of you have an accountability group?

6. Do you or your husband have serious depression or addiction of any kind? Are you seeking professional help?

9

Don't Let Differences Be Devastating

I believe every couple that marries has some extreme differences. Most of the time those differences attracted you to one another in the first place. However, those differences can begin to wear on each other's nerves as the marriage progresses. These differences have been known to cause separation and eventual divorce. A couple has to be willing to go to Jesus about those differences. The Word of God can teach a couple how to become flexible and forgiving with one another.

In order to understand differences better, a couple must be willing to openly communicate, without being demeaning or patronizing. All good marriage books stress that communication is the key to a happy marriage. One book in this area is *Communication: Key to Your Marriage* by H. Norman Wright. Learning to communicate is an art. Most of us have to work at learning this art. Learning how to listen is often more important than learning how to talk, and these books cover the topics well.

The book *Creative Counterpart* by Linda Dillow addresses the issues of men's and women's differences. With scriptural teaching, Linda explains how God intended for the male partner and female partner in the marriage to be different, and thereby to complement and complete one another. God created the two sexes to be different so that each could grow and learn from one another. If we both thought and acted alike, our marriages would be awfully boring. By getting in touch with our Lord's design, our marriages can become a resplendent radiance of His love.

One reason Gene was attracted to me was my desire for neatness and organization. One of the reasons I was attracted to Gene was his masculine strength and agility in sports. Through years of marriage, however, the original attraction in these areas has produced some friction. I really enjoy keeping a clean house, but Gene wouldn't say cleaning house is something he enjoys. We have had to reach a compromise in this area. Because Gene knows that cleanliness is important to me, he has learned to help. He helps me out by picking up his own clothes, keeping the garage clean, and repairing the household items as they need it. I have also had to learn to be less meticulous and let him just enjoy our home more.

I, on the other hand, do not get much out of watching a sports event on TV. Gene thrives on sports of any kind. At first I fussed and grumbled about the amount of time he spent watching sports. However, after sitting down and discussing it with him, I came to understand how important sports is to him. Sports is actually an extension of his masculinity, a vital part of his manhood, a recapturing and retelling of his youthful memories of victory and strength.

I, therefore, have tried to learn to enjoy sports as much as possible with him. Sometimes I even get excited about a basketball or football game, although I must confess that baseball still never gives me much of a thrill. Because I have the gift of mercy, it is difficult for me to enjoy men crunching or crushing each other out on a football field. I do enjoy going to a game and visiting with other friends who have come with their husbands, watching the cheerleaders, the band; and I have learned the more I know about specific players, the more I enjoy watching them.

Because I love my husband, I work at making myself sit down and watch a game on TV with him. He likes for me to be there with him, even if I don't understand the mechanics of the game. I have learned to do my quilting or other things while I sit by his side and watch the game.

It really gives me joy now to see Gene relax and have fun as he throws himself into a sports event. I must also point out that Gene is considerate about not watching three games in a row. Sometimes we'll make a bargain and he'll say, "I'll watch this game and then we can watch your program together." Or often he will watch a game and then go to the movies with me to see a special feature. We are both learning to be each other's creative counterpart.

That is what marriage is all about, give-and-take. I can give Gene the time he needs for his sports because I know that he will give me the time I need for things I enjoy. His sports are just as important to him as collecting my depression glass is to me. Gene goes with me regularly on his day off to help me find just the right piece of depression glass to add to my collection. Most of us just need to become more "stretchable," to venture beyond our comfort zone and enjoy being together. Being more stretchable will allow us to be more romantic with one another.

Keep Him Guessing with Variety

Men like variety; so be mysterious, provocative, and creative in the way you dress and in the things you do together. God has given you an intuitive nature that helps you know what your husband likes, so make a concerted effort to fulfill those needs in unique ways. Make life exciting! Have little surprises that keep him guessing. Plan a night out for the children, turn on the answering machine, then lock the door. Dress in an alluring outfit one night when he comes home to dinner. Prepare a new dish to tantalize his appetite and serve dinner in the bedroom by candlelight. Enjoy the romance.

I must insert here that it takes two to make a fabulous relationship. When your children see you and your husband trying to please each other, you have given them tremendous role models. Then, more than likely, they will grow up to have a healthy relationship with their spouses as well.

Establish a Regular Date Night

Men and women often differ in their ideas about relaxation; and with the hustle and bustle of your busy schedules for the church, children, and jobs, relaxation is often not given priority time. Helping Gene find ways to relax became my number one task in keeping us on the road to romance. While he pastored in Porter, Texas, we went through four building programs and the church grew rapidly in every area. As the church grew, so did Gene's responsibilities. It was especially important that he have time set aside for his family and himself.

Establishing a date night was one of our best ideas. We often went to a romantic restaurant and then to the movies. We talked all through our meal, then arrived at the movie early and continued our conversation until the movie began. Willard Harley Jr., in *His Needs, Her Needs,* says each couple should set a goal of spending 15 hours a week together in meaningful conversation and recreation. Those date nights helped us catch up on our quota for the week.

A marvelous little book titled *52 Dates for You and Your Mate* by Dave and Claudia Arp lists several creative ways to have a date night. The photo date can be an entertaining night as you set the timer on your camera and pose together, wherever you are. You can be creative and dress up in different costumes if you like. If you don't have a timer on your camera, buy an inexpensive extension cable to trigger the camera for self-portraits. Then spend another date night assembling and labeling your funny pictures in an album.

The gourmet cooking date is a delicious way to spend an evening together. Take one evening as a date night to look through all those cookbooks you received as wedding gifts. I collect cookbooks, so it takes more than one evening for us! Choose recipes that are new and sound wonderful. Make out your shopping list and go together to the store for your special purchases. Be a little extravagant on your purchases because this is a special night. It will still be cheaper than going out to eat at a restaurant. Then rush home with your treasures and begin preparing the meal together. You might decide to eat on the patio that night. Laugh and allow yourself to act silly while cooking and enjoying your gourmet meal together.

A coupon date can be fun for an extra 30 minutes here or there when your schedules are full. Half the fun of dating is the anticipation. These little coupons will give you something to look forward to doing together. Use your imagination and brainstorm ideas for the coupons. Then write on little colored squares of paper the things you decide. It could be watching the sunset together, flying a kite, roller skating, going for a walk, going on a picnic, or meeting at the ice cream parlor or coffee shop. Punch a hole through the coupons and tie them with a string. Hang those coupons in a conspicuous place, the bathroom or kitchen, so you will see them often. Talk each week about which coupons you can use that week. Try to use all the coupons within two to three months and then make some new ones.

The music date can be soothing to frazzled nerves as well as your ears. Many cities have music groups that give free concerts in the park. Check your local newspapers for free music recitals. If you live near a college or university with a good music department, check with them for a listing of free or inexpensive recitals and concerts.

Game dates can bring back memories of when you were first married and loved to play games together. If you don't have any games, go together to your local toy store and buy some. The games do not have to be expensive. These games can give you many hours of fun dates and happy memories.

The yellow brick road date is adventuresome and can even be educational. On these date nights decide to take a leisurely, scenic drive down a road you've never traveled before. You'll be amazed at what you might find: a park, museum, nature trails, antique shops, or a bed and breakfast. You may want to just get out of the car and sit and appreciate God's creation as the sun sets.

Friday nights were our date nights. Gene put it on his calendar and would not allow anything else to be scheduled on that night. Gradually, the people of the church learned that Friday night was just for us. It was a great testimony for other men in the church and their families as well. It has meant so much to me to know that Gene faithfully kept that night reserved just for me, no matter how much he was pressured.

An essential rule for these special date nights is to think and talk about the positive. If you have problems that need to be worked out, do it another time. Go on a marriage retreat, see a marriage counselor, or take another more serious time to work out your differences. Your dates should be reserved strictly for fun and relaxation. Don't bring up past offenses. You need to compliment one another the entire evening. When more time is spent in praise, more time will be spent in love!

Treating your spouse as you did when you were dating is a vitamin for your marriage. It will help put the pizzazz back into your marriage if it seems to be a little flat. Fifty years later you'll look back and say, "That was the best thing we ever did for our marriage."

Discussion Starters

1. List some specific ways you appreciate or can learn to appreciate your husband's sports and interests. What are some ways he has learned to appreciate your interests?

2. What are some ways you can keep your husband guessing with variety in your dress, food preparation, and attitude?

3. Do you have a regular date night? When is it? Where are some places you have gone? Which date night ideas are good for you and your husband?

10

Looking Your Best

As Jim, the new minister in the church, introduced his wife, Alison, to the congregation, you could see his chest swell with pride. Her gorgeous auburn hair glistened as it softly framed her face, and her deep, green eyes sparkled as the congregation clapped at her introduction. She appeared poised and friendly as she gracefully turned toward the congregation in a lovely rust-colored suit draped with a stylish scarf. Her complexion was radiant, and her demeanor exuded confidence mixed with graciousness. The congregation was thrilled to add to its family a woman who had a lovely appearance and was easy to get to know.

Alison had not always been this way. As a matter of fact, just a year ago Alison had felt drab, ordinary, and unexciting. She had always worked hard in the church in many areas. Everyone knew what a diligent worker Alison was. She had also worked in a bank during her husband's seminary days to help put him through school. Then the children started coming; there were three. It seemed that she never had a spare moment for herself. Between her home, the children, her part-time job, and the church, she never had any free time.

Then her cousin from Atlanta came to visit for a week. They had not seen each other in years. Her cousin Betty was a minister's wife too. She had come to town to attend a seminar. The first thing that caught Alison's eye when Betty stepped from the plane was her appearance. Betty was the same age as Alison, but Betty looked 10 years younger. And the clothes and colors she wore made her look gorgeous!

Alison had always felt that she was being vain if she spent too much time on her looks, so her appearance had received little attention over the years. But, Alison had noticed lately that Jim was paying less and less attention to her. She also saw more lines in her face every time she looked into the mirror.

That day in the airport as she stared at Betty approaching her in confident, graceful strides, she couldn't help but say a silent prayer, "O Lord, I would love to look that great!"

As Alison shared her home with Betty that week, they talked about their families, relatives, and their husbands' work. They were like two sisters making up for lost time. Finally Alison decided to put her pride aside and ask Betty how she managed to stay so beautiful.

"Oh, Alison, thanks. The right makeup and hairstyle make a big difference. They can take years off your appearance."

"But, Betty," chimed Alison, "your clothes always look so terrific on you. The colors are so perfect for your complexion. I wish I knew how to dress like that."

"Alison, you have so much natural beauty. It won't take much to bring it to the forefront. You just need a little help. We get help in every other area of our lives—medical, spiritual, intellectual. Why shouldn't we get some help with our appearance as well? Let's face it, as ministers' wives we are often seen as representatives for our husbands and their ministries."

With Alison's inner desires finally out in the open, Betty proceeded to head Alison in the right direction so she could get the help she needed to accentuate her positive features. All she needed was a few people who had the expertise to explain the importance of color selection, help her with her wardrobe and figure, and show her how to do her makeup and hair.

Before Betty left that week, Alison had vowed to herself to lose ten pounds and to begin a regime of beauty and good health. It was really the first thing she had done for herself since her wedding. She figured it was about time to start caring for herself, since she had spent the last 15 years caring for everyone else. What she found out later was that she was helping her family too because they were proud of her new look.

In a matter of months everyone in the church noticed a drastic change in Alison. The first change was her hair. Alison had thick, healthy red hair, but she didn't know what to do with it; so she pulled it back in a bun. A beautician helped her decide on a style that flattered her face and showed off her beautiful auburn hair. Then the beautician showed her how to style her hair herself during the week. Everyone at church raved about Alison's new hairstyle. With such positive reinforcement, Alison was encouraged to continue her beauty regime until she got the results she was looking for. The regime wasn't that difficult. As a matter of fact, it really was a lot of fun, and the results spoke for themselves.

The final reward came that morning at their new church when Jim introduced Alison to the congregation. "And now let me introduce you to the most beautiful woman I know, my wife, Alison!"

What minister's wife doesn't dream of being introduced by her husband like this? What minister doesn't enjoy introducing his wife when she is radiant and poised. Every husband desires to have a wife who takes pride in the way she dresses and looks. Every child, especially a teenager, wants a mother who looks nice and knows how to handle herself.

No matter how you may want to get around it, the way you look makes a striking first impression upon everyone you meet. The minister's wife has a unique position because she not only represents her husband in certain situations but she may also represent the church. For these reasons, it is important that you look your best.

Have a color analysis. It is a lot of fun and can help you

understand how your skin color and the colors you choose to wear can work to complement your appearance. Wearing the correct colors will give you a soft radiance.

I have a friend whose best colors are plums and muted colors. The plum color deepens her eye color and makes her look fantastic. Her clothes are not expensive, but she always looks striking because she knows how to wear the right colors in the right way. Be a woman who enjoys colors and wears them magnificently! Check your local library for a copy of *Color Me Beautiful* by Carole Jackson. She has a great way to find out which colors are right for you.

To make the most of our beauty, we need to learn how to enhance our features with the correct skin care. Learning how to subtly highlight your features is an art. Every woman looks more vivacious with a little makeup. Like that old saying, "Every old barn can use a little paint." Feeling good about yourself is what it is all about. Try enlisting a professional or even a talented friend to help you achieve your total look of loveliness. Many department stores have makeup and clothing consultants who are glad to give a makeover free of charge.

Find a good hairdresser, one who will look at the shape of your face, the texture of your hair, and consider your lifestyle. A stylish, carefree hairstyle is invaluable. It keeps you looking good and saves you time as you dress each morning. It goes a long way in giving you added confidence.

I hate to exercise! It is a constant battle; but as I get older, the results are rewarding. Beauty is not just putting paint on the outside; there is much that must come from within. Fitness is an essential part of looking your best. Find an exercise program that you enjoy and stick with it.

Spending a little time on your wardrobe will save you money. Don't be a slave to fashion; instead find a style that fits your figure, personality, and lifestyle, and stick with it. If possible, try to buy quality clothes during the off-season so you can purchase them reasonably. Hang your clothes in your closet according to color. That way you know what will go with what. Anne Ortlund in her book *The Disciplines of the Beautiful Woman* suggests only having some basic outfits in your closet. She also suggests making a list of everything that goes together and posting it in your closet so you can select some outfits on a moment's notice.

Just like Alison, taking pride in your appearance will give you a boost, and you will notice compliments such as, "Wow, you look sensational, honey!"

In this chapter I have focused on why it is important to look your best, beginning with you and then for your husband and also as a representative for your church. The suggestions I have given are for some a starting point, for others a refresher course. But this chapter would not be complete if I did not conclude with the point that beauty comes from within. No beauty treatment can create or radiate a Christlike spirit from within you. Beauty that comes from within far outshines any outward beauty.

We have all witnessed the woman who appears plain when we first meet her. However, after getting to know her, she seems to radiate with an inner glow that transforms her appearance. She has become one of the most radiant women we know. Her sweet, caring spirit, her gentle and positive ways bubble from within. This is the kind of beauty that comes only from spending time with God. He alone can make any woman radiantly beautiful. Resting in Him for our needs, following the commandments in His Word, and loving others as Christ loves produces an inner glow that is attractive to all who know you.

Discussion Starters
1. Have you ever had your colors analyzed? Are you a spring, winter, summer, or fall?

2. Are you satisfied with your makeup and its application?

3. Are you pleased with your hairstyle? Does it fit your features and your lifestyle?

4. Have you found a clothes style that flatters you? Do you have an organized closet? Do you have your closet arranged according to colors?

5. Do you take pride in your appearance? Are there ways you can improve?

6. How much time do you spend on being inwardly beautiful?

Part 3

A Joyful Haven, Not a Headache

11

The Tranquil Home

We all fantasize about a perfectly run home, but in reality there isn't one. Even homes with all kinds of help available have their problems. The Lord is the Helper Who makes the biggest difference in our homes. One of the most important jobs of a minister's wife is to make her home a haven and a place of peace and harmony. Home should be a safe place to find love and repose. Because your husband's job often deals with people's problems, or problems of the church, he needs a place away from the hectic decisions of his day, a place where he can get refreshed and recharged. In a society filled with constant confusion, noise, and interruptions, this is no small task.

It takes great skill and attention to achieve a restful place for you, your children, and your husband. When you add extras like caring for aging parents, and many times two careers, you almost need a miracle to accomplish the essential task of turning a home into a tranquil haven.

Share the Work

Through trial and error I have learned several things to get organized. First, write down all your duties in a day, in a week, and in a month. Then number those duties according to importance. Next pray over the list and ask the Lord to show you which items could be handled by another member in the family. It is amazing how much our children can help us if we train and encourage them. There will be many things on the list that only you can handle; but dusting, doing the laundry, cleaning the bathrooms, and vacuuming can all be handled by children. Teenagers can prepare some simple meals for the family, help a younger brother with his homework, and sort and fold the clothes. When the teenagers get older, they can even go grocery shopping and run errands.

You and your husband need to share jobs. Discuss what each is willing to do around the house. When the children see the two of you sharing responsibilities, they are more likely to follow your example. The jobs may not be done as well as you would have completed them, but learn to be a little less perfect and life will be easier for everyone. The wise minister's wife has to learn to be flexible and innovative. When you start your family off with the idea that all have important jobs to do to make the family run smoothly, life can be enjoyable.

Putting up a poster with everyone's jobs on it can be helpful when the children are young. Give stars or other rewards on the poster when the children complete their chores. When they are older, give an allowance as a weekly reward for their jobs. If the jobs are not completed, no stars or allowance. As the children get older, privileges can replace the stars and the allowance can hopefully be increased. The right motivation is the key. Remember to thank your family for their part in managing the housework. Compliment and brag on your children for a job well done.

When your husband arrives home after a full day's work, he usually needs some wind-down time before he is ready to interact with the family. It is helpful if you can give him this time. Fifteen to 30 minutes gives him time to change into some comfortable clothes, watch the news, read the paper, or whatever he likes to do for relaxation. When the children were very small, I tried to make sure that they were in bed by 7:30 each night so that Gene and I would have some quiet time together. That was our catch-up time.

When our children were growing up, each of them played an instrument in the band. Sandy played the flute; Eddie, the trumpet; Vicki, the clarinet; and Ty, the drums. We could have had our own band. However, it was very distracting to Gene when he came home to hear them all practicing their instruments at the same time. Therefore, I tried to make sure they all finished their practicing before Gene came home. I also attempted to have all the children studying quietly in their rooms when Gene first arrived home. They could come out of their rooms and give him a hug, but then had to go back to their homework and finish it before supper. When the children became teenagers, their schedules weren't so predictable.

Fathers Are Important

A father needs to spend quality time with his children. It's important that he play with them and read them stories when they're young. When they become teenagers, Dad should have a date night with daughters once a quarter. He needs to play sports and attend sports events with his children and get involved in their interests. If a father does not learn to spend time with his children, the children can become bitter. Your children must always know that Dad puts them before anyone else. The Lord can help you and your husband produce this balance through effort and prayer.

Use the Answering Machine

When your family has a opportunity to eat the evening meal together, turn on the answering machine so you are not interrupted. It is important that you guard the small amount of time your family has together. Using the answering machine can greatly assist you in this endeavor. You also may want to turn on the answering machine when you are visiting with each other, playing games together, watching a special TV program, or any other activity that draws you together as a family. Don't feel guilty about using the answering machine; that's what it's for. If the call is important or an emergency, then you or your husband can return the call quickly. If the call is not urgent, it can be handled at the office the next day. The children will be grown and gone soon enough. It is important to guard that precious time with them at home.

Home Life Must Receive Top Billing

Even if there are no children in the home, time between the minister and his wife is still important. You can easily become jealous if your husband spends a great deal of time away from home and then spends time on the phone when he is at home. This type of behavior tends to make you feel like a second-class citizen. When a wife feels like she has to play second fiddle to everyone who needs her husband's attention, look out, trouble is ahead!

If you feel this way, sit down with your husband and have an honest talk about your needs as a wife. Let him know that you need to spend time with him on a consistent basis. Having a consistent home life full of love, peace, and meaningful conversation does not just happen. It requires effort and prayer, but it can be accomplished. However, both the minister *and* his wife must desire to put home life at the top of their priority list.

In spite of the magnitude of the task of turning a home into a haven, the Lord will give you that ability. However, there is one thing you must do for the Lord, and that is to make time to talk with Him. I will share ideas on how to do that in the last section of the book.

Discussion Starters

1. What methods do you use to make your home a safe hideaway for your family?

2. Do you work outside the home? Do you have children? What are their ages?

3. Have you ever listed all your important activities in a day, a week, and a month that help you keep your home running smoothly?

4. Do you encourage your children and your husband to assist you with these activities? What reward system do you use?

5. Do you use your answering machine to cut down on incoming calls while the family is together?

12

Gracious Hospitality

Hospitality in the Rural Church

Frowning, I spouted at Gene, "What did you just say? How many people are coming to our home in 30 minutes?"

"Oh, it's just a meeting for the youth leaders, Virginia, about 10 or 12 people. A small group. They don't care if the house is clean or not," was his nonchalant response.

"They might not care, but I do," I retorted, bewildered that Gene had given me *so much* notice. Instantaneously, I saw dusty furniture and dirty clothes everywhere. What a mess! In the meantime, my esteemed man of God was oblivious to my concerns. It was as if he had on blinders and had tuned out the world. He certainly could "See no evil, or hear no evil!"

"It's really no big deal," snorted Gene. "I just got busy and forgot to tell you that they were coming over today."

"It may be no big deal to you, but it sure is to me. From the appearance of our home, those youth workers will think I won the slob of the year award!"

The wild-eyed, pale expression on my face conveyed that panic was setting in, so Gene reluctantly agreed to vacuum and pick up his things, while I cleaned the kitchen and baked some cookies.

Deal made, we both got into high gear and breathlessly

cleaned, polished, and generally threw our untidy abode together in astonishing order. As the door bell rang, Gene slammed the vacuum cleaner and dust rag into the closet. Momentarily frozen, we looked at each other and sang out simultaneously, "They're here!" Hurriedly grabbing the rest of the dirty dishes, I threw them into the dishwasher with one drop shot. Vibrations echoed inside the machine as I sprinted to answer the door.

We straightened our clothes and greeted our guests as poised as possible. But in the back of my mind I was making notes for future discussion. The matter of *advance notice* for company coming was absolutely going to receive a new definition! It eventually did!

This situation was repeated several times at the beginning of our ministry, with a few variations, of course. It took me years before I learned the lessons of being a gracious hostess. Much of it happened through trial and error. I had to learn how to make a home for our family and still allow our home to be used for the church and other ministry activities. That wasn't always easy. Over the years I learned to receive company into our home with a measure of grace. Now I love it!

Because we lived so close to the church, it finally dawned on me that our home was expected to be an extension of the church for meetings and youth gatherings. Having been married only 3 or 4 years, I still wasn't a terrific cook or housekeeper, but I was a fast learner. God had given me a knack for organization, so I was able to gather up some scrumptious cookie and cake recipes that I could whip up on the spur of the moment before a group arrived in our home. With a few housecleaning tricks, we made it through most hurried preparations for guests and committee meetings.

Many churches are known for their fellowships and their dinners on the ground. (For those city dwellers, I too had to learn that this didn't mean actually eating dinner on the ground; it simply means serving dinner outside on tables. A little matter of semantics.) At these important gatherings, I allowed my taste buds to do the testing, scouting around for the best recipes available. Usually recipe in hand that very day, I ran home and placed it in my recipe box. My recipe box is now two boxes, with luscious recipes from all over the nation, many proudly penned with the name and date of that generous giver.

If you are not in the habit of writing the name of the recipe giver and the date you received the recipe on the recipe card, begin now. It will bring you years of pleasant memories and sumptuous feasting.

Many times it is expected that the minister and his family will entertain a visiting evangelist, vocalist, or missionary. He or she will often spend the night in the minister's home and eat several meals with the minister's family. In our ministry in Porter, Texas, it seemed as though there was always a new face sitting around our dinner table. We also encouraged the children to have their friends over; and, of course, they ate with us too. I grew to love having visitors stay with us and fellowship around our table. However, having extra mouths to feed did require purchasing our groceries with care and economy. Planning is the key.

I first planned my menus for two weeks and I then made a list of items needed. I shopped at a wholesale store and tried to pick up only things that were on my list. Next, I went to the local grocery store for the small or unusual items that I could not get at the wholesale store. I tried to go to the store only once every two weeks because the more trips I made to the store, the more I spent.

When I returned from shopping, the children helped me prepare everything for the next two weeks' menus. Because most items were purchased in bulk, they had to be divided into portions. When I purchased a special item for a recipe, such as whipped cream, I usually had to announce to everyone, "Now don't eat the whipped cream because it goes with the strawberry shortcake we will have Sunday." Generally the kids were great in cooperating. Every once in a while an ingredient for a recipe came up missing and *nobody* ever knew what had happened to it. We had a family joke that "Mr. Nobody" ate the ice cream or hid the potato chips. He was the most active member of our family.

When I made a casserole for supper, I usually tried to prepare two and put one in the freezer for another meal or an emergency. I posted the menus on the refrigerator so everyone knew what we were eating that week. This also helped to eliminate the "What are we having for dinner tonight?" question each day as the children came in from school. All I had to say was, "Look at the menu." Posting the menu also helped in case I was late getting home from an appointment. All of the children knew how to cook; and if they had to, they could whip up that night's dinner without too much effort.

With constant visitors in our home and a family of six, who all had healthy appetites, it was a necessity to have good food available and lots of it. There are many good books on the market that teach you how to purchase and prepare in two days the menus for a whole month. Then all you have to do is add your fresh salads and vegetables and you have a wonderful meal in minutes. I wish I could say that I mastered this routine, but I must admit that some weeks worked out better than others.

Hospitality in the Urban Church

Some urban churches expect the minister's home to be opened to them for special occasions. Usually, in urban areas, people do not drop by unexpectedly. However, the minister's home should be available. One special time to invite guests into your home is at Christmas. If you and your husband are not too busy with children or other activities, this may be the year to have a Christmas open house.

When Gene and I were in Porter, Texas, we loved having an open house each Christmas for the church members. Christmas has always been my favorite time of the year. I delight in decorating the house in fresh evergreen and red bows. I was not working outside the home then, so I had more time to bake, prepare, and decorate. I began my baking in November and froze many of the desserts. Several women in the church helped with the baking. Sometimes different Bible classes can help prepare recipes for you as well. It is also nice to enlist women to help serve, keep the dishes washed, and help with the guests. Sometimes teenagers can tackle this task. With this kind of help, it frees you and your husband to visit and extend a warm welcome to everyone who enters your home. It's also a good idea to enlist a few women who have a flair for decorating to help decorate prior to the big event, unless you would rather do it all yourself.

If your guest list is long, schedule specific times for groups to come, either alphabetically, by class, or by organization. This ensures a smoother flow of guests arriving and leaving. Gene and I neglected to do this one Christmas and the entire congregation came between 3:00 and 5:00! I didn't get to see half of the guests because we suddenly ran out of coffee, punch, and cookies. I missed most of my guests because I was supervising the kitchen!

If you have small children at home, plan to have an adult or teenager available to play with them in their room. Even better, arrange for them to have a fun outing with friends during part of the day. If there are teenagers in the home, find out what they would like to do that day. Some teenagers might enjoy helping for a while, but eventually they will want to do their own thing with their friends. Don't expect your teenagers to act like little adults. Plan to let them participate in an activity outside the home that day too, something that they can look forward to with a friend. It will save you lots of frustration in the long run if you spend just a little time and effort planning for your children's needs, whatever age they are! I had to learn this the hard way!

If you do not have the gift of hospitality (that means you do not look forward to having people in your home, or you do not enjoy preparing for and serving them. And let's be honest, we don't all have that gift of hospitality.), then enlist several women who do have the gift of hospitality to help you.

Don't feel like your home must always be perfect before you have guests in your home. It took me a number of years to learn this. Guests remember your warm and caring spirit long after they leave your home. As long as your loving spirit welcomes them, they won't care if your floors aren't spotless. Many a minister's wife has turned herself into a wreck trying to make her home impeccable. Remember, the true sign of hospitality is love, not cleanliness.

Special Times for Hospitality

Staff fellowships provide a great opportunity to have guests into your home. This is a time when just the ministry staff and their families get together for a meal or refreshments in order to fellowship and get to know each other better. If you have a patio, outside fellowships are great too, especially for the children. Just plan simple meals such as hamburgers, hot dogs, and homemade ice cream. Use paper plates—the strong ones.

In larger ministries or churches the staff is so big and busy that special effort must be given to cultivate and maintain these friendships. Often these fellowships help the wives develop a support group. We tried to get together with all the staff for a Sunday meal after church at least once a quarter. We had the meal in a different home each time. The hostess provided the meat and drinks, while the other staff families brought the vegetables, bread, and dessert. There is something intimate about being in a home. You feel closer to that family after having been in their home as opposed to eating in a restaurant. You begin to feel like family and a close bond of love and acceptance develops.

Some ministers' families like to have the leaders of the church in their home for a meal at scheduled times. One minister's wife in Redlands, California, Jan, maintains a management and teaching career in a hospital, raises her children, assists her husband in witnessing, and sings in the choir. Needless to say, Jan is a busy minister's wife and has little extra time.

Even though Jan is a busy woman, she and her husband like to have a different church group in their home for a meal once a quarter. She purchases a prepared lasagna and cheesecake. She tops the cheesecake with fresh fruit and prepares a fresh salad and French bread. The meal is a smash. It doesn't require a lot of preparation, and everyone enjoys being in their home!

You don't have to prepare everything from scratch. There are many wonderful dishes that can be purchased, even from your local deli. It is not necessary to tell anyone that you didn't bake it yourself—that is, unless they just come right out and ask you—and then you can just smile sweetly and keep them guessing.

When you have friends or groups over, keep the menu simple. Relax and enjoy your guests. That way they will remember not only your good food, but especially your warm and friendly manner.

Discussion Starters

1. Do you and your husband have a compatible arrangement about advance notice when he invites people to your home?

2. Do people drop by unannounced? How do you handle it?

3. Do you have the gift of hospitality? If you do not, but know you need to entertain guests on special occasions, are you willing to enlist other people to help you?

4. Do you have a list of good menus to prepare for your family? Do you shop by planned menus? What great recipes do you have to prepare for special times with guests?

5. Do you have the ministry staff or church members in your home? How often? Do they seem to enjoy themselves and you? Do you enjoy them?

13

Prepare Your Home for Guests

As a minister's wife, people will always be in your home for one reason or another. Here are some tips to get your home ready for company and keep it that way. Before you are ready to receive guests into your home, you may need to spruce up your home a little. Emilie Barnes in her book *More Hours in My Day* tells about a little trick. Enter your home as if it were for the first time. Enlist a good friend to assist you in this task. Scrutinize the entrance of your home and the room where guests will be asked to sit.

Enter your home slowly and note anything that seems out of place, dirty, or in need of repair. Take a pad and pencil with you and write all these items as you notice them. Then spend at least 15 minutes each day cleaning out the clutter and dirt and adding personal touches.

If your company comes into the living room or family room, arrange the room for conversation. Have plenty of pretty coasters for coffee and tea. Make the room interesting and pleasant. Coordinate your color scheme, remembering that soft colors produce peaceful feelings. Place some personal items in the room, such as pictures and mementos to make the room more intimate. Baskets of ivy or greenery are a fresh touch.

It is not important to have new furniture. It is essential that the room reflect your personality and beauty. This room should offer a warm hug to everyone who enters, and your smile and sincerity will make them feel right at home.

If you need moral support, ask a friend who has an eye for color and fabrics to help you in your project. Sometimes the job can be overwhelming for just one person, especially if you are not adept at decorating.

Take a special look at the guest bathroom. Keep it clean and pleasant! If your guest bathroom also has to serve as your child's bathroom, then you have a real challenge on your hands. Train your children to pick up their dirty clothes and towels when leaving. It does take a little effort, but it can be accomplished.

Establishing certain habits in your home will save you time and energy. My father used to say, "A place for everything, and everything in its place." If you get in the habit of putting things in a certain place, then usually you will be able to find them later.

No matter how hard you try to put everything in place, it seems as though certain things are always getting lost. One August our oldest daughter, Sandy, got her driver's license. We were getting ready for company and discovered that we needed a bag of ice. Sandy volunteered (like all new drivers do) to go to the store for the ice. I gave her some money and my car keys and told her, as usual, to drive safely. She returned with the ice and immediately put it in the freezer.

That night after our guests had left, I remembered that Sandy had never returned my car keys. She looked in her purse; they were not there. She looked in her room; they were not there either. Everyone began a search all over the house for those keys! We looked under couch cushions, behind furniture, in drawers, and in and around the car. Those keys were nowhere to be found. How could those car keys just disappear?

We continued looking for those keys for months. Finally, we just gave up. One day when Eddie, our oldest son, was getting some ice cream out of the back section of the freezer, guess what he found? You guessed it. Sandy had the keys in her hand when she slid the bag of ice in the freezer that day. The keys slipped out of her hand into the back of the freezer all in one smooth movement. To this day, if anything is missing in our home, we all smile at one another and say in unison, "Look in the freezer!" Putting things in the right place in your home is helpful, but not always possible!

After you have everything in place and all the guest areas decorated, then it is time to pay attention to the most important room in the home. No, it's not the kitchen. It's your bedroom. Invest some time and thought on your bedroom. Gene and I have visited hundreds of homes over the years. It's amazing to me how many of the master bedrooms are catchalls for anything and everything in the home. For some reason, women spend a lot of time decorating the children's rooms, the kitchen, and living room, but they ignore their own bedrooms. This somehow reflects the erroneous idea that they don't deserve to spend money on themselves. They often feel that they can use the money somewhere else more beneficial. Not necessarily so!

You may think, *Well, no one else comes back here, so it's all right to leave these things laying around here. It doesn't really bother anyone.* A wife always needs to be on the lookout for new ways to express her love to her husband. Cleaning out that bedroom clutter might be one great way! Get another bookcase for the books and find a big attractive basket with a lid to store the magazines. Better yet, go through those magazines and throw away most of them. Evaluate the furniture that you want to keep in your bedroom. Only keep the essential pieces. With the right touches, it will require only a small amount of money to turn a plain bedroom into a comfortable hideaway. If you don't have money for wallpaper, put up a beautiful border. And if a border costs too much, find the right stencil and stencil to your heart's content.

The focal point in decorating your bedroom should be your bed. Keep the coverings simple, but beautiful. You don't want to take a lot of time making up your bed every morning.

A beautifully decorated bedroom, lavished with color, intimate treasures, and wonderful fragrances can be so inviting and comfortable after a long, stressful day. You will be pleased with the results.

Getting your home ready for company is not that difficult when you have a plan. Use the help of a decorator or a friend who has a knack for decorating to get you started. Give yourself about 15 minutes a day to accomplish the transformation of your home. Get your family to help. If you need additional help, budget for a housekeeper. Before you know it, you will look forward to welcoming guests in your home as much as they look forward to coming

Discussion Starters

1. Have you examined your entryway and living room lately for attractiveness and comfort for company? Is there anything you can do to make it more appealing?

2. Do you manage to keep the guest room and bath clean for your company? How do you manage it?

3. Do you have a system for trying to keep your home neat? What is it?

4. Do you have a helper who comes in regularly to assist you with your cleaning if you work outside the home?

14

Ḥandling Sudden Visitors in the Ḥome

When Gene ministered in Denton, Texas, he helped the members build a new parsonage right next door to the church. After the parsonage was complete, it was nice for Gene to walk only a few steps to the church each day from our home. However, living so close to the church produced some problems because people often stopped by unannounced. I was working full time, so Gene and I had few hours to be alone. Juggling quality time together, our jobs, school, and our church required a Houdini act. After a number of years, however, the Lord gave us the skills to handle these interruptions with grace and spend time together.

When you live close to the place where you serve, it requires a skillful minister and wife to carve out time for each other. One of the qualifications for a minister and his wife found in 1 Timothy 3:2 is hospitality. Hospitality is important. However, balance between hospitality and home life is important. You probably already spend a great deal of time away. Only you know how much time you have available for visitors and how much time is needed for the solitude of your family. It is up to you as wife and mother to be sensitive to your family's needs. You are the thermometer in the home. You must check your family's temperature for the need for togetherness, conversation, play, laughter, and rest.

No matter how wonderful the people you minister to are, there are always people who take advantage of the generosity and good nature of the minister's family. When you run into these well-meaning people, a plan of action must take place.

Because some people have no sense of time, it is up to you to be the timekeeper. Keep an accurate personal calendar of all your engagements. Write down your big and small engagements, like time needed to cook supper, to take the children to their appointments, to bake cookies for Vacation Bible School, to return correspondence, to organize a prayer group, or even to call your mother at a certain time! It is amazing how many appointments a mother and minister's wife can have in a day.

When your guest (announced or not) arrives, be as cordial to her as possible during the allotted time you have. You must decide how much time you can give her in your busy day. After giving your undivided attention and being aware of your time limits, stand up and let her know how glad you are that she came. Apologize for cutting the visit short. Explain that you have another appointment and that you must get ready for it. Slowly escort her toward the door.

Most people will understand and not monopolize your time any longer. She does not have to know what the appointment is. You can have any number of appointments with your beautician, your dry cleaner, your postman, your gardener, your husband, or another friend. It may just be an appointment to take a little nap before the children get home from school. Only you know your limitations and what it takes to complete everything in your day.

Be nice, but firm. Do not allow her to trap you at the door for another 15 minutes. Kindly insist that you must go and pleasantly begin closing the door while you smile sweetly and thank her for coming by. If she brought you something, thank her for her gift and be sure to send her a thank-you note. I believe the Lord wants us to be honest and kind with our words. As soon as she leaves, keep your appointment, whether business, friend, or a nap!

If she calls before she comes, be sure to candidly let her know if it is a convenient time or not. If it is not, politely explain that you are in the middle of a project or another appointment and arrange for another, more suitable time for her to come. Once again, try to be honest. If you arrange for her to come that day, tell her that you have another appointment at such and such a time, so a *little* visit would be great. This way she knows what the time limits are for her visit. Remember, little children in the home have big ears. Don't say negative things about your guests. Be sensitive about what you say about these unexpected guests. Scheduling your time with visitors is important. Be kind, but wise, and keep your sanity!

If you have the gift of counseling, people will often be at your doorstep for comfort or advice. Appreciate the opportunity to help another, but never let it interfere with the privacy of your home life. If counseling becomes too frequent at home, talk with your husband about the possibility of a support group sponsored by your church. You could be involved with the ministry, but not solely responsible. If the Lord leads you and your husband to another place of service, ministry will go on without you. Remember, you and your husband cannot save the world by yourselves. The Lord doesn't expect you to.

Lady Bird Johnson, wife of the former President, was noted for her lavish hospitality in her home after her husband's death. Everyone who wanted to visit her was given an opportunity. It seemed she never turned anyone away. Everyone who came into her home was so impressed with her sincerity and attentiveness to them. What most of them did not realize was that she was also a punctual person. She gave each person a full 15 minutes. During that 15 minutes she gave them her undivided attention and concern. But when the 15 minutes were up, she would rise slowly and very graciously thank them for coming. Then she would escort them to the door. No one felt slighted because during that limited time she was so accommodating and loving. I think many ministers' wives can learn a lesson from Lady Bird Johnson.

Knowing how to protect your family from too many visitors is important. With all the violence and disruption in our society, it is so important that we make a home that remains a haven for us and our family.

Discussion Starters

1. Is your home close to your church or office? Do you live in your own home or the church's parsonage?

2. Do you have a problem with people stopping by your home unannounced?

3. Do you have a system for handling these unannounced visitors?

4. Do you ever find yourself helping others more than you help your family?

5. If you adopted Lady Bird Johnson's technique for handling visitors, do you think it might help your situation?

15

The Home and the Wise Woman

Ministers' wives come in all sizes and shapes. They are all important and all special to the Lord, no matter what they do or where they live. Many work outside the home; others do not. Some have been to college; others have not. Some are mothers; some are not. If you and your husband do not have any children, you may be a mother figure to other children. God sent just such a woman to my husband when he was just 5 years old. All the children called her Mrs. Ruthie. For years Mrs. Ruthie, having no children of her own, taught and loved the 5-year-old department in Sunday School as if they were her own children. After becoming an adult, Gene found out that six young men from her tiny Sunday School class became ministers. How God used this dynamic woman!

When Both Have Prepared for Ministry

Some ministers' wives have completed college and received a seminary degree. They have spent a great deal of time and money preparing to serve the Lord. After receiving a degree, they are committed to serve God faithfully.

When you and the man you love have both prepared for ministry, how do you deal with career decisions and family?

How do you decide what to do about your career, your family, and your service for the Lord? It is not always an easy decision. I believe the Lord gives us different callings for different times in our lives. Rarely today does anyone keep the same occupation for the rest of his or her life—especially a minister.

Deciding to have a family is difficult for some women because, although they want to have children, they also want to fulfill the commitment to their vocation. Make it a matter of prayer. If God wants you and your husband to start a family, He will give you the peace and ability to be a good mother and wife. He will show you how to continue your ministry and raise your children at the same time.

Your ministry doesn't stop because you are at home. The focus of your ministry changes, but it is just as important. One of the waves of the future is contract work. It is amazing how much can be handled in our homes today with a computer, fax machine, and a phone. You can minister to the families your neighborhood or your children's school. There is a great need for ministry in our communities today.

The Minister's Wife Who Works Outside the Home

Many ministers' wives have no choice but to work because of financial reasons. When that is the case, I believe the Lord has a job designed that will enable a wife to stay connected to home and in touch with her family. As you pray about your career and financial situation and commit it to the Lord, He will open up avenues that you never dreamed possible. Ask some other Christians to pray with you about your situation and God will begin opening just the right doors.

The book *Mom, You're Incredible!* by Linda Weber explains the many tasks and expectations that mothers have in their lives. They are often overwhelming. When we commit our vocations and finances to the Lord, it is remarkable the miracles that He can perform. Claim Philippians 4:19 (NIV), "My God will meet all your needs according to his glorious riches in Christ Jesus."

Regardless of your educational background, your vocational choice, or your finances, God intends for you to put your family first. The years of actually rearing your children are so short compared to the years when they are grown. Make these years of raising your children count for the Lord. In doing so, they will actually count for you too. Your husband and your children will "arise and call [you] blessed" (Prov. 31:28 NIV). What more could a woman ask?

Is More Time Being Spent in the Church Than at Home?

It is very easy for the minister's wife to get wrapped up with constant ministry activities and church programs. That's why it is important for both you and your husband to sit down and prioritize the events for each week. Small children need the stability and love of a regular home schedule. Teenagers do too. Your husband's attitude in protecting you will go a long way in keeping others from enlisting you to head every committee or participate in every program. Gene was great in this area. When he accepted a position, it was understood they were employing him. I was his wife and the mother of our children first and foremost. I had my hands full just managing our home and keeping it running smoothly. He assured the committee that I would use my gifts in the areas that I felt led, but he didn't want anyone putting any pressure on me just because I was the minister's wife. I really appreciated his protection because it freed me to be a more responsive wife, mother, and homemaker; and it gave me time to find my place of service using my gifts and talents.

When the minister is protective of his wife, it simplifies her life and allows her to be what God wants her to be, not what others expect her to be.

Discussion Starters

1. What attributes do you use every day as a mother? Do you feel that others belittle your position as a mother?

2. Do you work outside the home? How many hours a week do you work? Do you find it difficult to manage your home and your time at work? Do you have outside help to assist you?

3. Did you attend seminary? Did you have a ministry or career before you married your husband? Do you feel fulfilled now?

4. What specific ways do you make your family your top priority? Do they realize that they are your main concern in life?

16

Raising Ministers' Kids

An important part of being a minister's wife and serving with your husband is knowing how to raise your children to love the Lord and not to feel bitter towards ministry. We have all seen ministers' children who had nothing to do with religion when they became adults. There are many factors that cause this type of behavior. Thank the Lord, many of these adult ministers' kids do return to the Lord later.

Is Too Much Time Being Spent in the Church?

Be sensitive to your children's needs. Sometimes, when too much time is spent at the church, a child may act out his or her frustration by becoming mischievous or rebellious. Through prayer and dialogue, a parent can find out if this is the root problem. If it is, then more time and attention should be spent at home. Often, if a parent is willing to skip just one meeting to stay home with the child, it will do more good than buying him or her all the ice cream in the world. It will produce an indelible confirmation of your love and devotion toward your child that he or she will never forget.

Children need to know that their mother and father love them and that their activities are just as important as any committee meeting in the church. Make happy memories in your home and don't become a slave to the ministry. "They [our children] will know us by our love," and our love begins at home.

Don't Expect Your Children to Act Like Adults

When raising your children, try not to say they must be good because they are a minister's children. If you bring your children up thinking they are supposed to be perfect because they are a minister's children, you are setting yourself and them up for a disappointing fall. Teach them from God's Word how God desires all children to behave and why.

Be careful not to put your children in a mold and don't let other people do it either. Remind people that you have children who are growing and learning. Remember that children make mistakes while growing up; that is part of the process of growing. We all made our share of mistakes and your kids will be no different. Try to surround your children with people who are great Christian role models.

Help your children find God's special plan and purpose for their lives. Teach them Jeremiah 29:11 (NIV) and show them how it personally applies to their lives. "'I know the plans I have for you; . . . plans to prosper you and not to harm you, plans to give you hope and a future.'"

Let them see you reading the Scriptures and praying daily. Tell them about how God teaches you and disciplines you in your daily walk with Him. This will make a deep impression on them.

Let them hear you call out their names in prayer. Let them see that God is an integral part of your life, not just on Sunday morning or Wednesday evening. Help them see God's blessings and His love for them individually.

Learn to Laugh at Life's Mishaps

Encourage your children to laugh at life's mishaps. In Proverbs it says that laughter is good medicine. Medicine is used to heal wounds. We all receive emotional wounds just by living. No matter how good a mother you try to be, you will make mistakes and feelings will be hurt. Laughter can help heal those hurts. Laughter will help your children know you are human and that you can enjoy life.

Have a humor contest once a month and judge who has the funniest joke or story. Do silly things around the house such as a backwards dinner (dessert first and the blessing last). On April Fools' Day short-sheet everyone's bed to end the day on a funny note. Cut out cartoons and hang where they will get a laugh. Let your kids make up a funny play and videotape it and send a copy to the grandparents.

When the children were young, I always instructed them not to spill their drinks while at the dinner table. One evening we were invited to eat dinner with the chairman of the deacons. I rehearsed the children's manners for them as we drove into the deacon's driveway. The four children dutifully listened to me, saying, "Yes ma'am," at the right cues. They had my little speech memorized. As we sat down at the table with the deacon and his wife, I eyed my little brood to make sure they were sitting properly at the table. They were. Then after the blessing, I reached to pass the dish of green beans, and over went my glass of tea. I was so embarrassed. All my children looked at each other and then at me, and in unison said, "Now, Virginia, don't spill your tea!" They thought it was so funny!

A wonderful book that can give you some terrific ideas about raising your children for the Lord is Kathie Reimer's book *Thousand and One Ways to Help Your Child Walk with God*. This is a very practical book that can assist any mother. Psalm 127: 3–5 (NKJV) says, "Behold, children are a heritage from the Lord, the fruit of the womb is His reward. Like arrows in the hand of a warrior, so are the children of one's youth. Happy is the man who has his quiver full of them; they shall not be ashamed, but shall speak with their enemies in the gate."

Psalm 127 (NKJV) also says, "Unless the Lord builds the house, they labor in vain who build it." We have a little plaque hanging on the wall in our home that reads:

House and Home
A house is built of logs and stone,
Of tiles and post and piers;
A home is built of loving deeds
That stand a thousand years.

Providing the foundation of God's love is the best gift a parent can give a child. Children need to be taught about the love of God at an early age. When the children were young, we read Bible stories, had question-and-answer time, and had prayertime every evening. This prelude to bedtime began around 7:30, after they were ready for bed, and lasted until 8:30 or 9:00.

Their primer was a book full of colorful pictures from which the children learned in poetry form about the love and beauty of God. They learned of the sanctity of the home and of the necessity of helping in the home. Simple prayers and songs made teaching our children so easy.

Bible Characters Are Realistic Role Models

As the children grew older, I turned the story reading over to a different child each night. They made up their own questions for the rest of the family to answer. Most of our reading came from a book of Old Testament stories for children. I also used the *Children's Bible.*

The wealth of wisdom contained in those Old and New Testament stories developed character in our children. In Deuteronomy 6:5–9 (KJV) God explains how we should diligently teach our children: "And thou shalt love the Lord thy God with all thine heart, and with all thy soul, and with all thy might. And these words, which I command thee this day, shall be in thine heart: and thou shalt teach them diligently unto thy children, and shalt talk of them when thou sitest in thine house, and when thou walkest by the way, and when thou liest down, and when thou risest up. And thou shalt bind them for a sign upon thine hand, and they shall be as frontlets between your eyes. And thou shalt write them upon the posts of thy house, and on thy gates."

Share your testimony with your children often. Tell them how the Lord drew you to Him, how you asked Him to forgive you of your sins, and how His Spirit came to live inside of you. Tell them how your life has been changed because of God and how God speaks to you today.

It's important that your children know that God disciplines you when you do not obey Him. When children realize that their parents are being disciplined by the Lord, they are more apt to accept your discipline for them. Share the Lord with them when you rise up, when you lay down, and when you walk. Then, they will be eager to share with you when they are older. But remember, with all your prayers and Bible teaching, your kids are still going to make mistakes. That's life and it happens to all of us!

With our busy lifestyles today, it is difficult to make time for family devotionals. Make it a priority. Ask for the Lord's help as you make this commitment. He will bless your efforts. Teach your children the Word not only through the Scriptures but through your example.

Each Child Is Unique

Because each child is unique, raise each child according to his or her particular personality. Don't try to raise your children all alike or you will fail. Each child has a different gift mix, traits, and personality. Therefore, each should be treated according to his or her unique gifts, talents, and personality.

James Dobson's books can assist any parent with questions about raising children. *Dare to Discipline, The Strong-Willed Child, Children at Risk,* and *Preparing for Adolescence* to name a few, are excellent Christian books to read as you raise your children. With the Lord's help, you will be able to raise children who have a personal relationship with Christ, know their spiritual gifts, and use them in the body of Christ.

Discussion Starters

1. How much time do you spend with your children each night reading and praying?

2. What special Bible story books do you use with your children? What other helpful books, games, or videos do you use?

3. Name some specific qualities your children can learn from Bible personalities.

4. Explain how each of your children is different. Do your children enjoy participating in church? Have they found ways to be involved in ministry projects they enjoy?

5. In what ways do you and your husband try to demonstrate love to your children on a daily or weekly basis?

17

Wounded Children, Healing Hope

Life is not always easy for the child of a minister. Growing up where eyes watch and judge your every move is an unpleasant experience. Some people will allow the minister's children to behave normally, but others expect the minister's children to act like angels. When the minister's child is criticized, that criticism can create wounds that last a lifetime. As the parent, you may need to run interference for your child.

Occasionally, someone will find fault with your child no matter how good your child is. If a disgruntled person criticizes your child, don't automatically apologize for your child out of embarrassment. Let your child speak and explain his or her side of the story. Carefully listen to both sides of the stories and then pray about the matter. Always gently, but firmly, let the person know that you will take care of the matter. Then ask if they will pray for your child. Set boundaries in love, and when the child steps over those boundaries, discipline in love according to *your* standards, not the expectations of others.

God can take an embarrassing and often catastrophic event in your child's life and work it for good. That is, if fellow Christians will covenant with you to pray for your child and not gossip about your child. When a fellow Christian agrees to pray for your child, it will be next to impossible for him to stay mad at your child. Your responsibility is to make sure there is action and nurturing along with those prayers.

If you let your kids be kids and give them your love, they will thank you for it later! Be reassured with Philippians 1:6 (NKJV) in regard to your children's Christian maturity, "Being confident of this very thing, that He who has begun a good work in you [your child] will complete it until the day of Jesus Christ." Do not let go of this verse for your children. Administer discipline fairly when necessary, but always possess unconditional love for them!

Hope Comes Through Prayer

Just about the time we received our children into our home, God sent me a precious book that greatly influenced my prayers for our children. It was Catherine Marshall's book *Adventures in Prayer.* This book emphasized the necessity of trusting in God for everything in relation to your children. Marshall related personal stories of childlike faith in praying and believing God.

Those stories pierced my heart and encouraged me like never before to claim the promises in God's Word for my children. It has been so beautiful to see God answer each one of my prayers for my children. They are truly the handiwork of God. Today as grown children, it is so wonderful when they call and say, "I really need you to pray for me about a problem I am having." Of course, that is my greatest desire. I want to intercede for my children, to bring their needs before my heavenly Father, fully aware that He loves them even more than I do.

A mother can have no greater assurance than to know that the Creator of all the universe is on her side protecting, loving, and guiding her children.

Evelyn Christenson in her book *What Happens When Women Pray* explains how she prayed for her children individually by name every morning before they went to school. What a marvelous and encouraging practice. Children need to hear their names being called out in prayer by their parents. Children need to know that their parents are always available to pray with them and for them in any difficulty they may have. What a great time we are going to have rejoicing in heaven as God shows us all the prayers He answered for us on our children's behalf!

Discussion Starters

1. Have your children ever done anything that embarrassed you or your husband?

2. Were you able to ask your fellow Christians to pray for your children because of the incident? If not, why not?

3. How do you normally handle disgruntled people? Are you careful to listen to your children's side? Do you allow the angry adult to intimidate you? Do your children know that they have your unconditional love?

4. What does Philippians 1:6 mean to you in relationship to raising your children?

5. Do you pray regularly *for* your children? Do you pray *with* your children? Do your children come to you, asking you to pray for them about particular needs? What prayers has the Lord answered for you on behalf of your children?

Part 4

Successful Ministry

18

Building Relationships

Because your husband is a minister, many will look up to him. A minister must always demonstrate wisdom and discretion.

Relationships can be all-consuming. Be alert to your husband's needs. Be as involved in his life as possible. Visit his office often and unexpectedly. Encourage him to avoid late-night meetings. If possible, accompany your husband on out-of-town trips. It's a wonderful time to have a little mini-vacation. If you can't go on a trip, call one another so you can share your day's events and express your love to one another. Gene and I have made it a practice to do this. Even Billy Graham calls Ruth every night no matter where he travels across the world. It is an ingredient that keeps a couple close, even if they are miles apart.

We must never underestimate the intentions of Satan—it is to kill and destroy. Our enemy will stop at nothing to accomplish his goals. Only through the combined prayers of the saints can this enemy be stopped. Ministers and their families need the constant prayers of their intercessors because Satan has targeted them for a fall. He knows that if he can ruin the life of a minister, he has negatively affected a whole community of believers.

Gene and I have six churches in Texas and several in California that pray for us regularly. We send them a list of prayer requests about every two months; more often if the situation demands it. We also call and talk to the prayer leaders and ask for their prayers over the phone if we need them. Try to find some praying churches. Make sure they can keep confidences and enlist them as your prayer warriors. You will be so glad you did.

Though a minister's wife should never show favoritism, it is perfectly acceptable for her to have friends. In fact, I believe it is absolutely necessary! God does not expect a minister's wife to keep herself aloof, never allowing herself to get close to others. A woman can understand another woman like no man ever can. Because women are basically different from men emotionally, psychologically, and physically, I believe women need to share their dreams, disappointments, and triumphs with one another. The Lord intends for women to uplift and encourage one another.

It is only natural that you will be attracted to some women more than others because of similar interests, talents, or children that are the same age. Do not feel guilty about having close friends. Gene and I witnessed a tragedy occur in a minister's family when the daughter became involved in a serious accident. Many complicated legal and moral problems developed because of the accident and the minister's wife went into deep depression. During this time, she seemed to have no real friends who could minister to her. It was sad to see that she had no one who could comfort and stand beside her in her time of need.

When trials come, and they will, friendships cannot be developed then; it is too late. It takes a close friend to stand by you in your day of trouble. Develop friends outside your husband's ministry as well. Make friends with non-Christians as well; they will come to your rescue in time of need. A minister's wife needs to develop friends during the joyous times, so when the difficult times arise she will be surrounded by love.

Always try to be kind to everyone by demonstrating Christlike love. But don't be afraid to have special friends around you. If your husband serves on a large church staff, sometimes a friendship can grow with one or two of the other staff wives. You already have a lot in common because of your husbands' ministry to your extended church family. If your husband is the only minister or works in another ministry setting, seek out a ministers' wives group or start one in your community. You can enjoy a time of fellowship and lift up one another in prayer and in love. Proverbs 27:10 (NIV) says, "Do not forsake your friend . . . , and do not go to your brother's house when disaster strikes you—better a neighbor nearby than a brother far away."

Develop Strong Guidelines for Behavior and Counseling

How a minister and his wife handle themselves in their ministry will set an example for the people they serve. A minister and his wife should always behave with discretion. Tainted jokes or lewd remarks are never Christlike for any Christian, but especially for a minister and his wife. Ephesians 4:29 and 5:4 (NIV) confirm this: "Do not let any unwholesome talk come out of your mouths, but only what is helpful for building others up according to their needs, that it may benefit those who listen. . . . Nor should there be obscenity, foolish talk or coarse joking, which are out of place, but rather thanksgiving."

Some people enjoy a big hug as a form of greeting. If this is the case, it is important that the hug never becomes more than a brief exchange. Ministers' wives should be especially cautious about this. A sideways hug (just putting your arm around the shoulder from the side) is acceptable. I try to hug women and extend a handshake to men. However, some men always hug no matter what. Acknowledge their sweet spirit and accept the hug graciously.

Be careful not to put yourself in a compromising situation. Try not to meet with a man alone and don't encourage compliments. A compliment is always nice, but anything more than that is unnecessary. Satan would love nothing more than to destroy your marriage, your ministry, and your husband's ministry through impropriety. Remember Ephesians 5:3 (NIV), "But among you there must not be even a hint of sexual immorality, or of any kind of impurity, or of greed, because these are improper for God's holy people."

Gene always followed four rules in counseling which kept him from the possibility of a compromising situation. First, he insisted that his secretary always stay outside his office when he was counseling a female. Second, he counseled a woman only during the day. If an emergency night counseling session came up, Gene always had me accompany him. Third, Gene established the rule that he never counseled about sexual matters. He felt there were specialists in this area who could handle that problem. Fourth, Gene always specified ahead of time that he would counsel a person (or couple) for only three sessions. If the person was not helped by the third session, he would refer that person to a Christian counselor. This way there was not the tendency for a person to become dependent on Gene to always solve his or her problems.

Gene developed friendships with several trusted psychologists in our area. If a person had not achieved victory over his or her problem after three sessions, Gene referred that person to a specialist. He of course continued to keep up with the church member's progress and offered them his concern and prayers. Some people had to continue sessions for over a year with a specialist before they achieved success in their lives. However, the right specialist made all the difference. It was a great plan. We saw many people come to victory from some serious problems in their lives. By using this referral plan, Gene was not tied down in extended counseling sessions. He could spend more of his time doing what he felt God had called him to do, preparing for worship and equipping the saints in the church for ministry.

Discussion Starters

1. Do you have close friends in your church? How have they ministered to you?

2. How do you deal with compliments and affection from church members?

3. Has your husband ever had a problem with a church member becoming dependent on him? What did he do about it? Has the problem been taken care of?

5. What kind of counseling rules does your husband have?

19

The Wrong Way to Resign a Church

It was the biggest fiasco! I had never been so embarrassed. Every eye glared at me as I sat in my pew at the church. What could I say? What could I do? "Just wait till I get my hands on Gene," I fumed!

Let me start at the beginning. Gene and I had served faithfully at this little church in Ida, Louisiana, while attending college. It had been a happy pastorate for over a year; but it had always been our plan to go on to seminary in Fort Worth, Texas, after finishing college. However, Gene had overlooked one small detail. He forgot to tell his congregation! This was his first church and he just didn't know how to break the news to them.

Once a quarter, Gene participated in National Guard duty on Sunday mornings. He always arranged for a visiting preacher on those Sunday mornings and was back in church preaching for the Sunday evening service. The day of the fiasco had been a National Guard Sunday. After Gene finished his National Guard duty that Sunday, he rented a trailer and brought it back with him to the parsonage which was right beside the church.

I couldn't believe he did it. Everyone was looking out the window as he drove by. He proceeded to park this rented trailer right in front of the church as we sat and watched.

It was like watching a movie in slow motion. We all saw Gene and his trailer pass by each of the sanctuary windows, and each time I winced a little more. I wanted to hide my face in my hands and shake my head, but instead I sat there frozen in disbelief!

When Gene and his trailer were finally out of sight, every eye in that church turned toward me. I couldn't blame those wonderful people for questioning this strange sequence of events.

If I could have melted into the pew and become invisible, I would have. But since I couldn't disappear, I muttered something like, "I believe Gene has something to share with you tonight." Boy, was I going to share something with him later—a piece of my mind! I knew that Gene was a young, inexperienced minister, but there was no excuse for this kind of behavior!

It seemed like a lifetime before Gene walked into the church. Then a blast of questions bombarded him. He tried to explain to the congregation as kindly as possible that the Lord was directing him to go on to seminary and complete his training for the ministry. It was a shock for the congregation, but they were very forgiving, considering the insensitive way their inexperienced minister handled his resignation.

As soon as we were alone, I informed Gene that if he ever resigned a church like that again, he would do it with his next wife, not me! Apparently, I made my point because Gene has always given at least one month's resignation notice to every church since.

There are times when it is best to resign a church. Here are some indicators that help you know when it is time to resign: (1) when the majority of the church doesn't want to follow the minister's leadership anymore; (2) when God gives clear direction to go to another location by opening doors (He will also give you and your husband a peace about the new situation); (3) when your husband senses God leading him into another area of ministry.

Gene and I have experienced all of these indicators in our ministry. We once went to a church eager to see souls saved and minister to the community. The community was changing and Gene had great ideas for ministering in it. It did not take long before Gene learned the leadership had no intentions of reaching out to the community. Gene and I were hurt, but since it was evident that they would not follow Gene's leadership in this important matter, we started praying that the Lord would open up other ministry opportunities for Gene. Within eight months after going to that church, Gene accepted the pastorate at another church. The new church generously followed Gene's leadership, and we stayed at that church for 11 years.

The time came when the Lord led us to resign that special church and go to another church in the Fort Worth area. We knew that the Lord had directed us to accept the new position in Fort Worth, but we really didn't understand why.

We had been at the church about five months. We still had questions about why God had moved us. One day Gene asked me to pick up a book for him at the bookstore. I had no idea that our little town outside of Fort Worth was so close to the seminary that Gene had graduated from years earlier. Following Gene's directions, I suddenly realized the bookstore was near the seminary. I decided to drive around the seminary and try to find the little house that we had rented while Gene was working on his master's degree.

As I drove around the seminary, the Lord reminded me of something that had happened almost 15 years before. When Gene had walked across the stage to receive his master of theology degree, something happened to me. It was as if the Lord tapped me on the shoulder and said, "Virginia, you and Gene will be back here someday." Distracted by the excitement of the moment, I looked up and said, "OK, Lord, whatever that means." Then I emotionally returned to the thrill of seeing my husband graduate. Later that week I was reminded by the Lord of His instructions and shared them with Gene.

Gene shrugged his shoulders and said OK too. He also didn't have a clue what the Lord meant because he was so glad to be out of school that at that moment he couldn't imagine going back. Years passed and Gene and I forgot about the Lord's words to us.

As I drove around the seminary that day looking for our old house, I felt the Lord tap me on the shoulder again and say to me, "Virginia, do you remember when I told you that you and Gene would be back here someday?"

I quickly responded, "Yes, Lord."

Then the Lord simply said, "Now is the time."

As I listened to the still, small voice of the Holy Spirit, my eyes grew wide with excitement and then full of tears at the possibility that the Lord had sent us here in fulfillment of His words 15 years before. I found the bookstore, purchased the book for Gene, and then rushed home to tell Gene about my experience with the Lord that day. "Darling," I said, "this answers our questions as to why the Lord sent us here. He wants you to go back to seminary!"

Gene listened intently and then said, "Virginia, I think you are right." He then told me about his luncheon meeting that day with Ebbie Smith, chairman of the missiology department at the seminary. They talked about Smith's latest book on church growth. Gene said, "In the course of our conversation he said I should enroll in the church growth doctoral program. He told me if I would get all the necessary papers together this weekend, he will do his best to enroll me with the next group of doctoral students that will start the spring semester."

We got all those papers together and Gene enrolled in the doctoral program. God continued to bless the church and He blessed Gene in school as well. In 2 years he completed all of his classroom work and was ready to begin his project. Then another surprise occurred in our lives. We were attending a religious convention one summer, eager to see friends who were serving in other locations across the country. In the midst of participating in worship, the Lord spoke to Gene and me again.

We were attending a commissioning service for missionaries. It was an inspiring service with a powerful message. All during the service, I felt a strong impression that the Lord wanted me to give my life to missionary service. I certainly was not expecting that at all! I had come to the convention to have a good time, not to be drawn by the Lord to consider a new area of service. I could not deny or ignore the Lord's wooing. I thought my heart was going to pound out of my chest, when I turned to Gene with tears in my eyes and said, "Gene, I can't ignore this any longer. I don't know why, but I believe the Lord wants me to give my life to missionary service!"

Looking into Gene's eyes, I could see that his were glistening with tears too. He gently took my hand and told me the Lord had been dealing with his willingness to surrender to missionary service all during this service too. Just then the preacher gave an invitation, asking all those who felt led of the Lord to give themselves to missionary service to come forward. Gene and I nodded at one another, took each other's hand, and walked down the aisle. We told the Lord that we would go anywhere in the world that He wanted us to serve.

As soon as we arrived home we received a call from California asking Gene to consider serving as director of missions in southern California. Gene laughed and replied, "Well, I just told the Lord that I would go anywhere in the world to serve Him and I guess California is part of the world!"

I immediately started praying that if it was not the Lord's will for us to go to California, the committee would eliminate Gene's name, quickly. He was one of 60 men being considered for this position and I didn't want to go through any long, drawn-out procedure if we weren't supposed to go. The committee finally narrowed the candidates down to 5, then 2, and ultimately Gene was selected as the man for the position.

Through our call to missionary service, and some events that took place in our church, the Lord showed us clearly that we were supposed to resign our church in Fort Worth and go to California.

So off to California we went to serve for nearly 5 years. The story of how the Lord directed us to resign in California and serve in Illinois is another amazing story for another day. Suffice it to say that once again the Lord made His will plain to us and we obeyed. It is a precious gift to have peace that you are in the center of God's will!

Resigning a church is never easy, but I hope your husband will use more discretion than Gene did the first time. Be sure to give plenty of notice and lots of love when you leave. Never say unkind things or leave with sour grapes, no matter how the church has behaved towards you or your family. You must always let the church members see a demonstration of Christlikeness in every situation. The testimony of your work and how you and your husband handle your resignation and move will live on for years after you are gone. Ask yourself if 10 years from now you can look back and be proud of the way you and your husband handled the resignation. We were proud of the words we spoke to our first little church; we just wished we had spoken them much sooner. So did the church members!

Discussion Starters

1. How many times have you and your husband resigned from a church or ministry position?

2. How much notice were you able to give?

3. Was your church understanding about your resignation?

4. Were there any resignations that could have been handled differently? How?

5. In what ways has the Lord directed you from one place of service to another?

20

A Daily Heavenly Encounter

Throughout this book I have referred to the need to take matters to the Lord in prayer. Prayer has been the foundation of my life. Without prayer I would still be that weak little girl, lost and wandering through life. It is prayer, the Word, and the Holy Spirit living within us that sets us apart from the rest of the world. It is spending time alone with God every day, studying and applying His Word that enables us to be a wife, mother, homemaker, and servant of the Lord. In order to be a student of God's Word every day, we need a plan of action.

First, you need to have a specific place in your home where you have your private Bible study and prayertime every day. You also must have a specific time for that Bible study and nothing should interfere with it. I believe early in the morning before your family rises is the best time. That way you start off fresh with God and ask Him to help you with your new day. When you rise before anyone else, the threat of interruptions is eliminated. When I was teaching school and raising our children, I would arise every morning at 4:45 so that I could have my time with the Lord.

The time I spent with the Lord each morning enabled me to teach high school, raise teenagers, and be a minister's wife.

I have set up a prayer notebook using regular loose-leaf paper. I combined suggestions from Anne Ortlund's book *The Disciplines of the Beautiful Woman* and Becky Tirabassi's book *Wild Things Happen When I Pray*. I have divided the prayer section of my notebook into two parts: my part and God's part.

In my part for prayer I have a section for praise to God. Each day I write several praises that deal with God's magnificent character. God's nature is worthy to be praised. I praise Him for His many facets of love and beauty. The next section is my thank-you section. Here I write all the things I am grateful for that God has lavished upon me. Writing down these thank-yous each day helps me stay positive about my life. It is amazing how many benefits God bestows on us and how often we take them for granted. The next tab under this section is titled "Admit or Confess." I try to write my areas of sinfulness and need for repentance. Repentance should be a regular part of our lives so that we can stay cleansed before the Lord.

Under God's part I have a section for listening. As I read my Scripture for that day, the Holy Spirit speaks to me and I listen. I often write the Scripture with the application for my life in parentheses. I study the Bible book by book, so when I am finished studying a book, I can take the notes out of my notebook and file them in my filing cabinet under the name of the book in the Bible. That way I constantly have fresh notes on what God has said to me from His Word. I also have a section for messages from ministers and another section for studies from Psalms and Proverbs. The last division under this section is for answered prayer. After the Lord has answered a prayer, I write down how the prayer was answered and the date God answered the prayer. Then I place that page in the back of my notebook under "Answered Prayer." It is gratifying to look back at all those answered prayers.

The next section of my notebook covers my requests. I have my requests divided according to the days of the week with a tab for every day. Every day I pray for my family and their needs. On Monday I also pray for people in ministry; on Tuesday I pray for extended family and friends; on Wednesday I pray for people who need salvation and the sick; on Thursday I pray for my personal needs and community and world needs; on Friday I pray for leaders in service; on Saturday I pray for other ministries and revival in our country. On Sundays I try to keep myself open to any new things the Lord may want to speak to me about and concentrate on worshiping and praising God.

I stay on task better when I pray like this. Divide your prayer requests up in such a way that they will meet your needs. You may have some different things that you feel impressed to pray for. The Watchman prayer organization also has a wonderful system of praying for one hour. Steps 1 through 5 tell you how to praise the Father, participate with the Father, petition the Father, receive pardon from the Father, and give proclamation to the Father. The important thing is to adapt these ideas so that you feel comfortable and you pray.

In *Prayer Shield,* C. Peter Wagner reveals that most ministers spend only about 22 minutes a day praying. Satan wants to keep us from spending the amount of time with our Lord that can make a difference. Korean pastors spend an average of 90 minutes a day in prayer. Most books on prayer emphasize that it is necessary to spend at least one hour a day in prayer.

I understand now why Martin Luther made the statement, "I have so much to do today that I must spend at least three hours in prayer." If you are not spending time in prayer, ask God to help you with the discipline of study and making Him first. Begin by making a covenant with the Father to pray 15 to 20 minutes each day. You will begin to see remarkable results!

I must confess that there are still mornings when I wake up and get caught in a barrage of events that prevent me from meeting with my Lord. On those days I greatly regret not being able to spend that coveted time alone with Him. When this happens, I try to go to bed early that night so I can start my next morning refreshed with the Lord again. If you are tripped up by Satan and do not spend your time with the Lord, do not spend the day berating yourself. Talk to the Lord as you go through your day and pledge to start again the next morning. We are all human and the Lord understands.

There is power in prayer! Mountains can be moved, minds changed, situations improved, and miracles performed through the power of prayer. I love the statement, "History belongs to the intercessors." I believe this is true.

The closer we get to the coming of Christ, the more we will see the power of prayer change our world. If you are known as a woman of prayer, you will also be known as a woman of power! God says, "Whatsoever you pray, believing that you shall receive it, it shall be done." What more power can a woman have than this—to be able to have top visiting and petitioning rights with the King of the universe? That's far better than holding even the highest office in the land.

One of the greatest prayer promises in the Scriptures is found in Matthew 7:7–8 (NIV): "'Ask and it will be given to you; seek and you will find; knock, and the door will be opened to you. For everyone who asks receives; he who seeks finds; and to him who knocks, the door will be opened.'" These are precious promises that we can claim daily.

Daily Duties

In that same three-ring notebook I keep a section for daily duties. This section helps keep my life organized and running smoothly. In this daily duty section I have one tab for calendars. Under this tab I print a copy of Gene's schedule for the next four or five months. I add my own schedule to his just to make sure we are coordinated. I have two more tabs for speaking engagements and letters to write. I keep my necessary notes under these sections.

Another tab is for books. Under this section I keep a running list of book titles and authors I recommend to others and books I want to read. Behind that page I keep a running list of any Scriptures or thoughts that I want to use in books I want to write. The last page under my book section is for the listings of books or tapes I lend out to others. I put the date I lend out a book or tape, the person I lend it to, and the title of the tape or book. That way I can keep up with all my books and tapes no matter where they are.

The last tab is for a journal. Here I write about the activities and events in my life. I don't do it every day; but when certain things seem important, funny, or interesting, I jot them down with as much detail as possible.

In that notebook I also keep stamps, extra stationery, and envelopes. Looking back over my journals through the years, I have seen God's hand in answering so many prayers. I have found it essential for me to have a prayer notebook so that I can remember everything the Lord wants me to pray for every day. Whenever a person asks me to pray for him or her, I try to write down the request wherever I am and then transfer that request to my prayer book as soon as I get home. That way I don't forget it.

I keep a small calendar in my purse. The calendar has three months in detail and a small 3-year calendar. I pull out my calendar whenever I think of something I have to do on a certain date and make that notation immediately. I keep a running list of things I need to accomplish each day and cross them off as I complete them. Whenever Gene asks me to do something for him, I pull out my calendar and write it down immediately so I won't forget. I couldn't operate without an organized plan of action. I have taken author Emilie Barnes's idea and put all my prayer items in a basket that I keep by my prayer chair. In my prayer basket I have my prayer notebook, two translations of the Bible, tissue, and pens.

I also keep a spiral notebook in my prayer basket in which I have started my own concordance with topics that the Lord has led me to study. I have listed topics from Angels to Waiting on God. After doing a thorough study on any topic, I am confident of God's leadership in that area.

If it is a beautiful morning and I want to go out to the patio to pray, I can just grab my prayer basket and go. Most of my praying is done in my prayer chair in the family room; but if I want to go to another room for my quiet time with the Lord, everything is together in my prayer basket and ready to travel.

Be a Prayer Warrior for Your Husband

Through the years of our ministry together, Gene has always depended on me to pray for him every day. God has put him on the cutting edge for the Lord; and, therefore, he has needed prayer covering his life. I count it a privilege to pray for such a powerful man of God. He, I believe, counts it a privilege that he has a wife who prays for him.

When you pray for your husband constantly, it is amazing what God can do with and through him. The more useful a man is to God, the more prayer he needs to thwart off the enemy. God will impress me at a specific time when Gene is going through an unusually rough period in his ministry to fast and pray for him. The combination of prayer and fasting is the most successful way I know to reach God's heart.

When we become totally dependent on the power of God through prayer, God works miracles in our lives that would not be possible otherwise. Only through prayer and obedience to God's word can we become what God created us to be. Oh, that we could learn more about the omnipotence of God and the mortality of man!

Discussion Starters

1. Do you have a specific time and place for prayer every day? Where and when? How much time do you spend in the Word? How much time do you spend praying each day?

2. Do you keep a prayer journal? How do you keep up with your prayer requests and needs? Do you list the answers to your prayers? How do you pray regularly for your husband and family?

3. Do you pray regularly for community, state, and world needs as well as people inside your church? Do you have a special group you pray with?

4. Do you spend time praising and thanking God every day for His goodness and benefits? What benefits are there to praising and thanking God every day?

5. What method do you use to keep your life organized? What kind of calendar do you use to keep up with your daily schedule?

21

The Secrets of Successful Ministers' Wives

I asked some ministers' wives who have lived long, happy, and victorious lives four basic questions: (1) What is your philosophy about being a minister's wife? (2) Were there any problems you had being a minister's wife? (3) What funny or embarrassing moment do you remember as a minister's wife? (4) What advice would you give a new minister's wife? I know you will enjoy reading their responses as much as I enjoyed visiting with each of these special women.

Margaret Hines

Margaret Louise Hines is a beautiful, petite, silver-haired woman in her 60s, sitting like a queen in her wheelchair. Her husband passed away 2 years ago. Margaret served faithfully with John for 47 years as a minister's wife: 7 years in Europe, 4 years in Germany, 3 years in Norway, and 33 years in California. Twenty of those years were in one church in California. She certainly exhibits the qualities of a woman of wisdom, grace, and beauty.

I asked Margaret her basic philosophy about being a minister's wife. She responded: "Always show love to the people in your church and you will receive their love in return. I always felt that if the people of the congregation loved me, they would love my husband as well. The last thing I ever wanted to do was be a hindrance to my husband, John. I made a special effort not to ever gossip in any way. I still get invitations back to our old churches. In each place we served together I loved the people dearly. In all our years of service, there was only one church that did not treat my husband properly. However, with prayer, God helped us to forgive them. We just couldn't hold grudges."

"Were there any problems for you, Margaret, being a minister's wife?"

"My biggest problem was feeling like I lived in a glass bowl when I was raising my children. I thought I must be perfect, spelled with a capital *P.* I thought the congregation expected me to be perfect. I was always worried that my children were not what ministers' kids should be. Finally, someone said something to me that made me laugh and see the reality of the whole situation, 'A minister's kid would be perfect, if it weren't for him playing with the deacon's kids.' Well, that statement set me at ease and I finally realized that no one was perfect!"

"What funny or embarrassing moment do you remember as a minister's wife?"

"Forty-two years ago John's parents belonged to Bristol Street Baptist Church. Pastor Long called and invited John and me to the dedication service for their new building. We drove to the church; and as soon as we arrived, I quickly looked for a rest room before the service began. Glancing at the sign, I rushed in. While still in the rest room, I heard the door open and someone else entered the room. You can imagine my surprise when Pastor Long walked in. We were both shocked. Pastor Long quickly apologized for coming in. Horrified and embarrassed, I didn't know what to say except, "That's OK." The pastor left quickly, and so did I.

"The new building did not have all the signs on the rest rooms and I had wandered into the men's rest room by mistake. Mortified, I ran out to our car to hide. The whole ordeal was so embarrassing I wouldn't even come in for the dedication service. John came out and tried to get me to come in, but I wouldn't budge. Finally, Pastor Long came out to the car and told me the story of his accidental entrance into the ladies' rest room. Well, he put me at ease, and I went inside with John for the service.

"Another funny incident occurred on Christmas. It had always been my job to handle the plays in our church. One December I was directing our Christmas play. Mary and Joseph had a quick scene with the manger, and then they were to freeze with a spotlight on them while the rest of the play continued on another part of the stage. The day the play was to begin we still needed a spotlight for Mary and Joseph. I rushed home to pick up the necessary props and spotlight and placed them in their correct places before the play began.

"Mary and Joseph finished their lines and then stood motionless in the light for about 30 minutes. As they stood, perspiration started dripping from their faces. I thought it was just a case of severe stage fright. After the play was over, Mary and Joseph complained about feeling flushed and hot. Further examination showed that they both had a pretty bad sunburn. My worst fear was confirmed when I looked closely at the lamp. I had mistakenly picked up my sunlamp instead of the spotlight. I felt terrible and apologized to them. They were very sweet about it, but they said they sure would check out what kind of lamp was shining on them from then on. We all had a great laugh. That Christmas they went home and dug out their suntan lotion."

"What advice would you give a new minister's wife?"

"Thank the Lord for the opportunity to be a minister's wife. Try to overlook little criticisms from people because it is just a natural tendency for people to criticize. Be sure to love the people and be there for them when they need you."

Frankie Pitman

Another special woman who served as a minister's wife for 15 years is Frankie Pitman. Frankie and Ellis have served in southern California most of that time, over 4 years in San Jose. She also served with Ellis when he was a director of missions.

"What did you enjoy most about being a minister's wife, Frankie?"

"I enjoyed doing what Ellis needed me to do. Because I am an introvert, I didn't need to be in the limelight. I enjoyed working in the background with all age groups. I loved being a true 'helpmeet.'"

"Frankie, what was the greatest problem you experienced in being a minister's wife?"

"Juggling all the activities in which I was involved. I participated in activities in the church using my gifts and talents. But I also participated in many other activities in the church, outside my gift range, to be supportive of my husband. It was difficult handling all those activities. I worked full time, all except 3 years while I was having babies. It was almost impossible to do it all: work full time, be a mother, wife (minister's wife), and a very active church member."

"What funny stories do you have because you were a minister's wife?"

"One year Ellis, with the help of the church, wanted to give me a surprise birthday party. Ellis told our son Kevin, who was 4 years old then, to bring Mommy to the front of the church when Ellis gave the signal. When Ellis gave the signal at the close of the service, Kevin grabbed my hand and proudly escorted me to the front of the church. Excited daddy and pastor asked his 4-year-old little conspirator, 'Kevin, why have you brought Mother up front?' Kevin looked out over the congregation, happy that he was the first one to proclaim, 'Because it's her birthday and she's 33 years old!' Well, I was surprised on two counts: that the church was giving me a birthday party and that now the whole church knew my exact age!

"Another funny incident occurred when Ellis began pastoring in San Jose. A special church member took care of our children during the day while I was at work. This woman was also a cake decorator and would often work on her cakes while the children enjoyed playing in her backyard.

"One day she was working on an exceptionally beautiful three-tier white wedding cake. Kevin, then 3, would run into the house for various reasons all through the day. When he came in, he would always stop and look with questions in his eyes at that white bridal cake.

"Finally, after about the tenth trip into the house, he stopped in front of the cake and looked up at the kind care-taker, announcing, 'I sure wish my father and mother would get married so they could have a cake like that!' Well, need-less to say, that story got back to Mom and Dad and eventu-ally the whole church. Ellis assured Kevin, 'We had a wedding and enjoyed a beautiful cake like that, but that was before you was born.'"

"What advice would you give a new minister's wife?"

"Pray often with your husband. Decide with each other what positions you feel God wants you to fill and don't allow yourself to feel pressured into trying to fill all the slots in the church. If you are not gifted in an area, do not allow your husband or a church member to pressure you into an area in which you know you have no business.

"The area of forgiveness is important. I have had a few people get angry with me in the past, but I have given that concern to God and asked Him to help me forgive them and then love them. By doing this, God has prevented me from becoming bitter.

"Your behavior at home is so important to your chil-dren's well-being and view of the church. You can't cut people up with your words and spit them out at home and then expect your children to love the church people and respect them. Try to always be positive about the church members around your children. They are smart creatures and they will imitate you every time."

Connie Powers

Another special woman is Connie Powers. Her husband, John, pastored in Tennessee for about 5 years. Then she and John moved to Beaumont, Texas. Connie answers these questions with her wonderful Tennessee drawl.

"What do you feel is your greatest asset as a minister's wife?"

"My relationships with people. I love people and I truly enjoy being with them. I have been told that I have a gift for making everyone feel at ease around me. I help John at 9:30 and 11:00 every Sunday morning at a special time to meet and chat with the visitors. I get to give each visitor candy hearts as a symbol of our love and the love of the Lord for them. I enjoy this because talking is really my thing. I enjoy having people in our home too. Entertaining is no problem for me. It's lots of fun."

"What do you feel is your biggest problem as a minister's wife?"

"Oh, that's easy. I hate to write thank-you notes! I have terrible handwriting and I'm self-conscious about it. I don't mind speaking to groups at all; but you ask me to write a note and I freeze up. So John and I have made an agreement. I'll do any speaking that I'm asked to do, as long as John will write the thank-you notes. It's a pretty good arrangement for us."

"Connie, what was one of your most embarrassing moments as a minister's wife?"

"I guess it would be right after we moved to Beaumont. The people of the church had been so gracious in helping us get our new home fixed up. One of the first Sundays we were there a special couple from the church came by to check on us and make sure we were all right. People were always stopping by to see if we needed anything in our new home. We had left a hose on in the yard to water the lawn since it was so hot. The couple looked so nice in their Sunday best. As they walked up the sidewalk, Nathan, our 6-year-old son, ran outside to help. We all came outside to greet our handsome visitors. Nathan rushed to move the hose so the woman wouldn't trip over it.

"While he was trying to move the hose, he accidentally sprayed water all over the back of her dress, right down to her heels. She was a soaked mess. She turned around to see who was squirting her with water. Nathan looked dumbfounded as he realized what he had done. She had a great sense of humor and started laughing immediately. Nathan then chimed in and we all had a good laugh. She had to rush back home to change her clothes before church, but she was so good-natured about it. From that point on I made sure that Nathan stayed away from that hose when guests came to visit!"

"What advice would you give a new minister's wife?"

"Know that God has put you together the way you are for a purpose. Even though you may look for a good role model for a minister's wife, don't try to imitate that person. God knows His plan for you and He has equipped you for that purpose.

"Remember that God has a great sense of humor. The ministers' wives I had known in Tennessee were quiet, soft-spoken women. When John, who was already pastoring, asked me to marry him, somehow I couldn't see myself as a minister's wife. I didn't fit the mold. I have a bubbly, chatty, sanguine nature. God has helped me to laugh a lot as a minister's wife and He has taught me to enjoy the person that I am. God likes variety and He certainly got it when He made me a minister's wife.

"Also, be a good steward of the gifts God has given you. Don't try to be a steward of someone else's gifts. Learn to say no when someone asks you to serve in an area that you are not gifted. Tell them that you would be taking the blessing away from someone else and you would be out of God's will."

Connie then shared another story with me that I think will help every minister's wife.

"I received a phone call from a woman in our church in Tennessee. For some reason this woman thought I had snubbed her at church. The woman proceeded to accuse and criticize me, causing me to question my service in the church. It really destroyed my self-worth. When I hung up the phone, I was in a state of shock, totally devastated by her criticism.

"I later found out this woman had a history of emotional problems; but the damage had been done. I was in an unusually vulnerable time in my life. Isn't that just like the enemy to attack you when you're down? I just couldn't seem to get over those cutting words. A dear friend in the church heard what had happened and noticed how depressed I was. One day she handed me something she had made especially for me. As she gave me the gift she said, 'I want you to hang this in your home and I want you to read it every day. Memorize every word of the verse until you really believe it in your heart. Remember, I love you and God does too.'

"As I memorized the saying [about being a child of God and being His special treasure] on that beautiful plaque, it became real in my life. The depression over those cutting words left me and I realized what a privilege it was to be a child of the King. I experienced true Christian love through a wonderful church member who was sensitive to my needs."

These are the stories of just a few women. I'm sure each one of you has some stories about your life as a minister's wife and about how much God has shone His love intimately on you.

Discussion Starters

1. What words of wisdom have you gained from the women in this chapter?

2. Do you believe these women have felt confident all the time about being a minister's wife?

3. What are some of the lessons in life that God has taught each of them?

4. Have you known any ministers' wives who have had a positive influence on your life? Who were they?

5. Do you think that you are being a positive influence on others as they observe your life in Christ?

22

Be a Joyful Team

"But, Lord, I am so different from Gene! How in the world will we ever be able to serve You together?"

Gene is a risk taker; he is full of conviction; and he has an insatiable desire to "grow" and "go." I, on the other hand, am a quieter, steady influence, intuitive and sensitive to people's needs. I am more in tune to balance, order, and creativity.

It took a while, but Gene and I gradually began to appreciate each other's differences. After developing some maturity, Gene and I realized that we were not supposed to think or act alike. In fact, our differences were an asset to our marriage and our service to the Lord. Every couple in ministry can complement one another. Because you are very different, those differences, when blended by God, will enable you to serve as a unique team.

Over the years Gene and I have learned to work together in some interesting ways. I enjoy helping Gene at the conclusion of every worship service. After Gene preaches a dynamic message, he usually calls on me to help counsel with people who come forward. I loved taking people back to the counseling rooms to help them with their problems or to lead them to accept Christ as their personal Savior.

The Lord has also used me to assist Gene with my gift of discernment. Whenever he has needed to hire a new staff

149

member, he has always asked me to spend some time with that prospective staff person. Usually we have gone out to eat. Because of my gift of discernment, I have been able to help determine if that person was the right one for the position. I appreciate the fact that Gene has always tried to listen to my evaluation. He sees my gift of discernment as a valuable part of our ministry together. The Lord has even used my love for English to proofread and type most of Gene's papers through his college, master's, and doctorate degrees. I sure have learned a lot in this endeavor.

Couples can work together in many ways in a worship service. Often the wife plays the piano and sings while the husband leads the music and/or preaches. For years this was the expected combination for a husband and wife in ministry. However, today, there are many other combinations that are just as effective and acceptable. Sometimes the wife uses her gifts on the sidelines by giving encouragement and strength to her husband as he stands in the pulpit to preach and as he ministers to the people.

Your husband's job can often produce a lot of pressure. He needs the stabilizing force of your love just to maintain his balance in the ministry. Gene depends on me to lift him up, encourage him, and especially pray for him. If you have the gift of exhortation, use it to help your husband as well as your church family.

Don't be misdirected by thinking your husband's ministry is your ministry. God has called him to serve using his gifts and talents. God has called you to be his wife using your gifts and talents in the body as He directs. As you serve the Lord together, the key is to use your gifts. As you use your gifts, you'll be happy and people will affirm you and your service.

There are many ways you can serve alongside your husband. Here are just a few ideas. If your husband is a minister of youth, you can go on youth trips, help with fellowships, and love and counsel young people.

People always appreciate a visit in the home or the hospital from the minister's wife. They always enjoy getting a card or a phone call from you. If you enjoy baking and have the time, people love a delicious dessert made just for them. I used to bake coconut pies or brownies for people in our church. I took the desserts to encourage them or to say thank you for their efforts on a church project.

We know the wife of a minister of music who not only leads all the children's choirs but also writes and directs the plays that are presented in the church. Another minister's wife, who is not musical, is known for the fabulous meal she prepares for the entire choir after their Christmas pageant each year. She also selects little individual gifts to give to every member of the pageant.

Many ministers' wives, who have the gift of teaching or administration, serve by teaching a Bible class or directing a department. I know a staff wife who does a tremendous job running the church library and video center.

Another precious wife has the talent of decorating. She has made gorgeous flower arrangements for banquets and has given beautiful arrangements as gifts. One staff wife, who has a marvelous talent for baking and decorating cakes, has baked the cakes for her church functions for years.

Some ministers' wives serve as their husbands' secretaries. Others enjoy having people in their home often because they have the gift of hospitality. All of these women have learned how to serve with their husbands using their gifts in their own way, working as a team.

When a wife is faithful in serving the Lord and is available to her husband, that alone speaks volumes. Your presence in your husband's ministry is of immense importance. Your presence and sweet spirit are a testimony. Church members need to see you participating in the church services and enjoying yourself doing it.

I must admit that there was a time when I wasn't able to participate in church as much as I wanted to. We were in the midst of raising our teenagers and I was teaching high school. Occasionally I had to stay home from Sunday evening service just to get regrouped and recharged. Because of my introverted personality, it was really a survival technique. It seemed that I had so few quiet moments in my life at that time. But, it was a point of frustration to my husband and to some of the church members. My husband would tell me how much he missed my being in the service. He said he needed me there for moral support. My mind wanted to be there but my emotions and body just couldn't always handle it. Of course, with Gene's sweet request, I tried my best to be in every service for him. Later, after the children were raised and I wasn't teaching school, it was easier for me.

The minister's wife who is raising young children should be excused from being in every service in order that she might establish a regular eating and sleeping schedule for her children. Small children should not be expected to stay during late services. Church should be a place you and your children enjoy, not a place you have to be because your husband is a minister. It is important that your children see you supporting your husband and loving the fellowship in the church.

Try never to compete with your husband in serving the Lord. Most opposites marry; and, therefore, have different gift mixes, talents, and personalities. Your gifts will complement and complete your husband's, just as his will complement yours. It is a wise woman who does not become jealous of her husband, but understands the praise he receives from others is an affirmation of her support in his ministry. After all, just by being his wife, you make him look better! Brag on each other's strengths to one another and to your friends. As you do this, God will solidify your partnership and help you to appreciate and enjoy one another more.

Gene and I have enjoyed serving the Lord together in so many ways. Through the years we have led seminars together, spoken to ministers and their wives as well as lay leaders and their wives, and facilitated marriage seminars. Not only have we worked together in these ministries but we also have helped each other in the home in encouraging and caring ways. You may not be serving directly with your husband today, but the Lord may allow you to do that in the future. I was busy raising our children and working full time for years, but later the Lord allowed me to travel and work more directly with my husband. All good things come to those who wait on the Lord!

Through the years Gene and I have used the word *minister* as a verb and not a noun. We have come to understand that every couple is to minister together wherever God has placed them. We are all called to minister using the gifts and talents God has given us!

Discussion Starters

1. What are some of the differences that you and your husband have in personality, gifts, and talents?

2. In what ways has the Lord used you to help your husband in the past?

3. Has your ministry together changed over the years?

4. Do you think you have to be in the spotlight to be used as a partner with your husband?

5. How has God used your differences as a couple to complement each other and make each other complete?

Conclusion

Discovering Indescribable Joy in Ministering Together!

In spite of my awkward and often embarrassing beginnings, becoming a minister's wife has turned out to be a beautiful experience. I fought serving with my husband for a while because I really didn't understand what it meant to give my life to Christ. I think there are probably some of you who have also been fighting the leadership of the Lord in ministering with your husband. I am speaking from experience when I say that the more you fall in love with Jesus, the more you will realize that serving with your husband can be great.

As you study God's Word and learn more about Jesus, you will begin to have a joy that is indescribable. That indescribable joy is Jesus!

As you spend more time in God's Word, pray more, and understand how much Jesus loves you, you will learn that ministers and their wives are ordinary people who are being used by God. They are not supersaints. Relax, be yourself, and let God empower you. Lose that halo. Don't try to be perfect. You'll just frustrate yourself and others. Keep those wings. It is the Spirit of God that empowers you to mount up on wings like eagles, that helps you to run and not grow weary, walk and not grow tired. Those wings will be His power claiming His promises that will enable you to soar through the clouds of discouragement to His sunlight of love.

While attempting to live the life of a minister's wife, Jesus will fill you with what you need. When you are filled with less of yourself and more of Jesus, His glory will shine forth from you. His glory will then attract others into His kingdom. Focus on the King of kings and the Lord of lords. May we follow the exhortation found in the age-old hymn "Turn Your Eyes upon Jesus": "The things of earth will grow strangely dim in the light of his glory and grace."

Now, may you go forth flying in His power and shining for His glory!

Epilogue

Dear Friends:

Since writing this book, the Lord has led Gene and me to the wonderful state of Illinois. We have found Illinois full of warm, sincere people who have exuberantly followed Gene's leadership as the state executive director of over 1,000 churches. It has been exhilarating to travel with Gene to different churches, sharing his zeal for the good news and his enthusiasm about reaching our communities for Christ.

God has used Gene mightily to cast a vision of evangelism and prayer before his staff and ministers across the state. They have embraced that vision, encircling it with their passion, and adopting it as their own. What a great work God is accomplishing in Illinois because His men and women are willing to press forward for the cause of Christ, no matter the cost.

I have been busy completing my master's degree in communication at the University of Illinois in Springfield. Gene and I love our home in Springfield. We live next to some of the nicest neighbors God ever created. All our children are married now. With excitement and pride we have watched them, with their spouses, bloom into beautiful, productive Christians. What a tribute to the Lord they are!

Most recently, trauma and seeming tragedy have enveloped our lives. Due to a reaction to an injection six months after prostate surgery, Gene was stricken with a massive brain hemorrhage. The hemorrhage was so severe that the doctors couldn't operate and they didn't expect him to live through that first night.

Shocked and bewildered, I waited in the hospital that night for what would happen. I couldn't imagine Gene's life ending this way. Then, softly and quietly, the Lord came to me and told me Gene would be all right. The Lord also said that He was going to work mighty miracles through this ordeal. They would have many ramifications that I wouldn't begin to understand. He told me to stay focused on Him and He would bring me through.

Now, some ten months later at the release of this book, those words from the Lord are still the best advice I have received. God's Spirit, His Word, and His people have been my rock and fortress. I wish I could say that my faith has remained strong throughout this journey; but every time I have faltered, the Lord has gently picked me up and placed me in the faithful arms of His Word. There He has tenderly fed me His promises, giving me the sustenance and strength I needed to carry on.

The details of this journey are for another time, but suffice it to say God has assured me He will have a special work for Gene and me to accomplish when He has brought us through this valley.

Seven months after the hemorrhage, after two and one-half months in a coma and three and one-half months in rehabilitation, Gene is home in Springfield. He is gradually improving, receiving therapy three times a week. Often he thinks I am his sister, mother, or daughter. Sometimes he remembers I am his wife. But regardless of who he thinks I am, he knows that he is greatly loved. God is healing Gene gradually every day.

I said this was a seeming tragedy. From the world's eyes our lives may appear nearly destroyed. But from God's eyes He is using this event to prepare us for an even greater battle ahead. God has promised me that, just like Jacob, Gene Wilson will be restored to be a greater witness for Him than he ever dreamed possible. The last chapter of our lives has yet to be written.

We all have a great cloud of witnesses in heaven who are cheering us on and saying, "Don't give up! It's worth the battle!"

"May those who sow in tears reap with shouts of joy. Those who go out weeping, bearing the seed for sowing, shall come home with shouts of joy, carrying their sheaves" (Psalm 126:5–6 NRSV).

We *shall* come again rejoicing, bringing in the sheaves!